a parent's guide to

8th Grade

Ensure Your Child's Success in School

Elizabeth Chesla

LEARNINGEXPRESS

New York

Library of Congress Cataloging-in-Publication Data:
Chesla, Elizabeth A.
    A parent's guide to 8th grade / by Elizabeth Chesla—1st ed.
       p. cm
   ISBN 1-57685-382-9
      1. Eighth grade (Education) 2. Education—Parent participation.
I. Title.
   LB1629.7 8th
   373.236—dc21

                                     2001033888

Printed in the United States of America
9 8 7 6 5 4 3 2 1
First Edition

Reprinted materials:
"Sleep Deprivation Among Adolescents" reprinted with permission from
www.cosmiverse.com, copyright © 2000; see pages 71–72.

"Those Days, Now These" reprinted with permission from Rachael Dudzic; see page 14.

Parent-Teacher Conferences; reprinted with permission from Home and School
Institute (HSI), copyright © 1989; see pages 131–132.

President's Challenge Physical Fitness Program; reprinted with permission from The
President's Challenge, copyright © 2001; see page 38.

"Sexually Transmitted Infections" (2001); "Helping Young People Delay Sexual
Intercourse" (1998); "Reducing Teenage Pregnancy" (2000); reprinted with permission
from Planned Parenthood® Federation of America, Inc., copyright © 1998, 2000, 2001
PPFA. All rights reserved; see page 129.

"Multiple Intelligences" from Frames of Mind by Howard Gardner. Copyright © 1983
by Howard Gardner. Reprinted by permission of Basic Books, a member of Perseus
Books, L.L.C; see page 77.

"Talking with Kids about Tough Issues: A National Survey of Parents and Kids"
reprinted with permission from the Kaiser Family Foundations, Nickelodeon, and
Children Now, copyright © 2001; see pages 133–34.

Test definitions adapted from www.fairtest.org; see pages 90-91.

For more information or to place an order, contact LearningExpress at:
   900 Broadway
   Suite 604
   New York, NY 10003

Or visit us at:
   www.learnatest.com

SEP 2008

Acknowledgments

Though writing is often a solitary task, it is by no means something one does alone. There are many people whose input and support made this book possible. Erik, first and foremost, thank you for your endless patience and support. Jennifer and Sandy, you got me started and kept me going, always on the right track. Marguerite Hartill, Kristopher Harrison, Barbara Lyon, and Dr. Timothy Dunnigan, thank you for sharing your expertise and giving me invaluable feedback. Jelena Matic, you have been a part of so many projects with me, and once again I am grateful. Finally, thank you, Lukas Jude, for inspiring me to be the best parent I can be.

About the Author
and Contributors

Elizabeth Chesla is a lecturer in English at Polytechnic University in Brooklyn, New York, where she coordinates the Technical & Professional Communication Program. She is the author of several study guides, including *Write Better Essays, 8th Grade Reading Comprehension Success,* and *Improve Your Writing for Work.* Elizabeth lives in New Jersey with her husband and son.

Dr. Timothy Dunnigan is a clinical psychologist and family therapist in San Diego, California. He is the author of *HELP for Families* and the online parents' guide www.helpforfamilies.com.

Barbara Lyon is the eighth grade guidance counselor at Taylor Road Middle School in Alpharetta, Georgia. She has been a middle school guidance counselor for over ten years.

Contents

chapter 1

Welcome to 8th Grade

ASK ANY group of parents or educators to describe their eighth graders, and you'll get a surprising—and often contradictory—range of responses. Eighth graders are often quiet and withdrawn, yet they're often loud and outspoken. They keep pushing you away, yet they're still deeply influenced by everything you say and do. They can make a perfectly reasonable argument as to why they should be allowed to date, yet they can't seem to understand your perfectly reasonable argument for why they should wait. They want to be individuals, yet they want desperately to fit in.

Welcome to the drama of eighth grade! Your child is now a full-fledged adolescent, and she'll experience profound physical, emotional, and intellectual changes during this roller coaster of a year. As she moves from childhood to adulthood, she'll begin to look like a young woman, and she'll begin to strive for the independence of adulthood, for which she's not quite ready yet. And with the onset of puberty sometime between the ages of 11 and 15, your teen will become a heap of hormones, undergoing changes and feeling emotions she won't always understand. As a result, she'll sometimes feel a little lost, sometimes a little scared, and often very confused as she struggles to figure out who she is and who she wants to be.

That, of course, is where you come in. As much as your eighth grader may push you away, as much as you may feel he doesn't want you around, *he does*. He wants you to be involved in his life. He *needs* you to be involved in his life. He needs you to know what's happening to him and around him, especially in school where he may face pressure to conform or try drugs and where he'll face a curriculum that challenges his developing reasoning skills. As the saying goes, "Little kids, little problems; big kids, big problems." And your big kid will need you to help him work those problems out.

This book is designed to give you information and advice that will help you be a more effective parent to your eighth grade child. The book aims to give you an understanding of the whole eighth grade experience—the emotional, physical, and intellectual changes and challenges your child will face this year. This first chapter presents an overview of what your eighth grader is going through on these three fronts while the rest of the book develops key ideas more fully and offers concrete strategies for being an involved and effective parent. The following chapters describe the eighth grade curriculum in detail, explain the stages of your child's social and emotional development, offer activities to supplement classroom learning, and suggest ways to develop a close relationship with your young teen. In addition, you'll learn about the benefits of extracurricular activities, the standardized tests your child will face in eighth grade, how to explore possible career paths and higher education choices with your teen, and where to find some of the best magazines, books, CD-ROMs, and websites for you and your eighth grader.

THE SETTING: MIDDLE SCHOOL

IN most school districts, students make the big leap from elementary to middle school in the sixth or seventh grade. "Middle school" is an appropriate term for these important school years (which in most school districts includes grades 6, 7, and 8 or grades 7, 8, and 9). As an eighth grader, your teen is in the middle of a whole lot of things: between childhood and adulthood, between elementary school and high school, between dependence and independence. In some ways, the structure of the typical middle school helps students through these difficult transitions. But that structure can also frustrate students who are struggling with developmental issues.

You already know from your child's sixth and seventh grade years that middle school is no longer the child-centered place that elementary school was. Instead of sticking with the same teacher and the same group of peers throughout the year (a practice called "self-containment"), middle schoolers may change classrooms (and therefore teachers and classmates) up to eight times a day. They have to navigate from class to class on their own, and they are expected to know where to be, and when, and which assignment is due for each class. In their typical day they experience a variety of teaching styles and a range of different expectations.

WHAT'S EXPECTED OF YOUR 8TH GRADER

IN eighth grade, your child will be faced with challenging courses that aim to prepare her for high school. Intellectually, your teen should now begin to approach problems systematically and think abstractly, and in school, she will be expected to be able to use these reasoning skills to analyze problems, make strong arguments, and explore abstractions. Your teen will also take important standardized tests during this year—tests that will show how your child's academic skills measure up against other students and statewide standards.

Though individual school curricula will vary, the typical eighth grade curriculum will expect students to attain the following knowledge and skills by the end of the year:

➤ **Writing.** Eighth graders will be expected to write narrative and persuasive essays that are well organized and that support a strong, clear thesis.

➤ **Literature/Language Arts.** Eighth graders will be expected to read and understand increasingly complex literature that often will be related to topics being covered in other classes.

➤ **Civics.** Eighth graders will be expected to understand the principles and structure of American government and the U.S. Constitution.

➤ **History.** Eighth graders will be expected to know the major events in the history of the United States through the twentieth century.

➤ **Math.** Eighth graders will be expected to solve introductory algebra and geometrical equations, interpret and create graphical representations of data, and understand and calculate probabilities and statistics.

➤ **Science.** Eighth graders will be expected to learn key principles of the physical, life, and earth sciences, including the structure of matter, the laws of force and motion, the basic principles of genetics, and the theory of evolution, and to know how to use the scientific method to solve scientific problems.

 FACT: Most "every day" texts, like newspaper articles, magazine articles, websites, and brochures, are written at the eighth grade reading level.

The eighth grade curriculum also includes art, music, and physical education, and may include foreign languages and electives.

In addition, by the eighth grade, students will be expected to take notes effectively, manage their time efficiently, and participate in class regularly and thoughtfully. Most schools will also expect students to know how to use both the library and computer to conduct basic research and how to use the computer for word processing.

These expectations can add up to a lot of stress for your child. Eighth graders are under pressure to master certain skills and knowledge at a time when their bodies and feelings are changing at an unprecedented rate. They're beginning to really feel the weight of the future as much talk begins to turn to high school and beyond. And their school day will often extend well into the evening with homework assignments that can add up to several hours each day. As a result, your eighth grader may become increasingly concerned with, and competitive about, grades and school performance.

While it's important to watch for signs of stress in your teen and to help him develop strategies for dealing with academic pressure, do keep in mind that people (especially children) tend to live up to what's expected of them. If your child's school has high standards and seems to expect a great deal, take heart. The more rigorous the curriculum, the better prepared your child is likely to be for high school, and the more likely he will be challenged to achieve his full potential.

Outside the classroom, your teen will have the opportunity to participate in all sorts of extracurricular activities, from band to athletic teams to computer clubs. These extracurricular activities are an essential part of the middle school experience—so beneficial, in fact, that some educators believe they're *as important* as the regular academic curriculum. These activities help reinforce academic and social skills and help develop important character traits such as discipline, responsibility, cooperation, and self-esteem.

CENTER STAGE: YOUR CHILD

THE leading actor in this drama is, of course, your child, who is changing physically and emotionally in many important ways.

A New Body

Between the ages of 10 and 13, most girls experience a tremendous growth spurt, often reaching 95% of their full height. By the eighth grade, most have also begun to menstruate—one of the most exciting and sometimes frightening rites of passage for females. They are now women who are capable of getting pregnant, and this change brings with it a new—and very serious—responsibility.

Sex Talk

Like it or not, eighth graders do a lot of thinking about the opposite sex, and most have probably already had their first "real" kiss. Some have begun experimenting with foreplay, and a few have even "gone all the way" by the eighth grade. (According to the National Campaign to Prevent Teen Pregnancy, *one in three* girls have had intercourse by the time they are 16 and two-thirds of boys lose their virginity by age 18.)

The best protection against unwanted pregnancies and sexually transmitted diseases is **information**, and the best person to give your child information is **you**. If your child knows the dangers, the responsibilities, and the joys of physical intimacy *when the time is right*, she'll have more respect for her body and be more likely to behave responsibly. And if she's heard this information from you and knows she can talk to you about these issues, she'll have more respect for you, too.

Boys typically take longer to finish growing (in fact, some boys don't reach their full height until they turn 20). But they still undergo dramatic growth in the middle school years, though their big growth spurts (sometimes stretching several inches in one school year) often come a year later in the ninth grade. Facial hair is probably a few years away for most, but not for all, and many will notice their voices begin to crack and then deepen in the eighth grade.

Body Image Rules

With all of the changes their bodies are going through, eighth graders are particularly susceptible to "body image blues." Bombarded with images of "perfect" supermodel and celebrity bodies, adolescents are likely to spend a lot of time fretting that they don't measure up—that their breasts aren't big enough, that they're too short or too heavy, that they're too "wimpy" to be attractive. Some worrying is natural, of course, but obsession with appearance can lead teens to dangerous territory, like anorexia, bulimia, or steroid use.

When teens suffer from the body image blues, it's important to help them be realistic about their appearance. For one thing, they're younger than most of the models and celebrities they admire, and they still have several years of growing ahead. And, along with growth comes a natural loss of "baby fat" that disappears with age. Also, supermodels and celebrities look the way they do only after lots of manipulation through make-up, lighting, camera angles, and retouching of photographs.

You can help your eighth grader by focusing on what's positive about his or her appearance and, more importantly, about his or her *attitude*. After all, looks may attract, but personality is what makes someone stick around.

Because different body parts grow at different rates, many eighth graders go through an awkward or clumsy stage where their body parts don't seem to match up and they seem to have trouble controlling their body. Hands and feet may seem too big for their arms and legs; their nose may seem too long or wide for their face; their teeth too prominent or eyes too closely set. They may trip over nothing and seem to be constantly knocking things over. Their body parts will soon catch up to one another, but in the interim, the awkwardness, like the acne that often accompanies puberty, can have a major impact on their self-esteem.

It's important for parents and teens to remember that adolescents mature at different rates, too. Some girls start menstruating as early as nine; others not until they are 14 or 15. Some boys begin to grow facial hair as early as the seventh grade; others not until they're off to college. Of course, your eighth grader will constantly be measuring herself against her peers. To keep a healthy self-esteem, she'll need accurate information about what's happening to her body and about how widely the ages for some of these changes can range.

Emotional Roller Coaster

The hormonal changes eighth graders experience can make them feel like they're on an emotional roller coaster. One minute your daughter may be feeling happy and carefree; the next minute, she may burst into tears. Worse, she might have no idea why. Similarly, your son, who is normally optimistic, may suddenly find himself feeling despondent for no apparent reason. Many teens know to expect the physical changes that come with puberty, but they may not know that their hormones can have a dramatic impact on their moods, too. It's natural, then, for your eighth grader to be extremely sensitive—and important for you to be extremely sensitive, too.

New Friends, New Attitude

The social and emotional changes eighth graders experience are as dramatic as the physical. After all, it's not only their bodies that are becoming more grown up. Eighth grade is a year of self-discovery in which teens are really struggling to figure out who they are. They desperately want to be independent of you, but at times they still need you just as much. This dependence will often frustrate them because they want to be more grown up than they really are.

At this age your child will also begin grappling with important moral issues. Your teen will likely be facing questions about premarital sex, drug use, and violence, and he'll know people (including some of his classmates) who are engaging in one or more of these activities. Your teen will need lots of guidance in navigating these complex issues and resisting peer pressure to participate.

Friendships and peer groups are particularly important for eighth graders as they develop a strong self-concept; after all, our friends help us define who we are. Friendships are often strong but may be fickle as teens discover more about themselves and search for others who share more of their interests. Kids who seem to be good friends can also be surprisingly cruel to each other. Because their feelings are so easily hurt, eighth graders will often hurt others as a kind of defense mechanism. And because they are so sensitive and so afraid of not being liked, they often try to protect their vulnerability by appearing tough or indifferent.

Spare Time Favorites

What do eighth graders like to do in their spare time? The top interests of the typical eighth grader usually include playing **sports**, listening to **music**, and using the **computer**. It's important to encourage your child's interests, which help him develop a strong identity and often provide excellent opportunities to develop important social skills. Even all those hours chatting online help your teen learn how to express himself and get along with others.

Your child's taste in **music** is likely to be very different from your own, but it deserves extra respect. Music can express emotions that your teen may be feeling but may not be able to articulate, and the music your teen enjoys may speak to her in a way that really helps her cope with those feelings. Take the time to listen to your teen's favorites and talk to your child about the music that moves her.

Eighth graders can be surprisingly rude, too. Many parents wonder what happened to their little angel who never talked back, who never questioned their authority. But this rebellion against authority—yours, their teachers', indeed any adult's—is an important part of an adolescent's social and emotional development. It's healthy (though you may find it awfully annoying, coming from your child) for your teen to ask why one person has the right to tell another what to do. Teens can't truly respect authority unless they understand it, and this kind of questioning can help them understand why people around them make the rules that they do.

In eighth grade, it's more important than ever to fit in, and you can expect your child's peers to exert a great deal of pressure upon her about everything from the clothes she wears to the music she listens to, even to the way she interacts with you and others in the family. She may seem to care much more about what her friends think than what you think. But don't be fooled—as indifferent as your child may seem to your input, your eighth grader is deeply concerned with what you think and feel.

BEST SUPPORTING ACTOR: YOU

Parents and families are the first and most important teachers. If families teach a love of learning, it can make all the difference in the world to our children.

—RICHARD W. RILEY, FORMER U.S. SECRETARY OF EDUCATION

Though you may often feel as if your eighth grader doesn't want you around, you are far more important to your child—and far more instrumental a factor in his or her success or failure—than you and your child may realize. Every day your child must make important decisions about how to handle academic and social situations. Every day your teen may face peer pressure to do potentially dangerous or destructive things. *Your* involvement in your teen's life is the best way to help your teen make the right decisions.

Being Involved at School

When parents are involved in their children's education, everyone benefits. Students get better grades, and, more importantly, they have a more positive attitude about school, about their families, and about themselves. By being involved, you will be able to better understand what goes on in your child's school and the pressures on and expectations of your child both in and out of the classroom.

Negative Attention

When children don't get enough attention from their parents, they often resort to bad behavior to get Mom or Dad to pay heed. This is as true of teens as it is of toddlers. They may know they're going to get in trouble for what they do, but they'll take that negative attention over no attention at all. Paying **positive attention** to your teen is one of the best ways to prevent unwanted behavior. Get in the habit of noticing what your teen is doing and offer specific praise when you catch your teen doing something right.

It probably seems a lot harder to be involved at your eighth grader's school than it did when she was in kindergarten. Opportunities for involvement, such as parties and field trips, seemed to come along regularly in elementary school; now they don't come along as often. But that doesn't mean there aren't plenty of ways to participate in your child's education. There are several things you can do, including:

1. **Read everything that comes from your child's school.** Know the curriculum, understand school policies, take note of activities that you or your child may be interested in, pay attention to issues that are being raised, and watch for opportunities to become involved, such as chaperoning special events or volunteering for school fundraisers.
2. **Know who is teaching your child** and what they're teaching. Meet your teen's teachers as early as possible in the school year; ask for meetings if they aren't regularly scheduled. Be sure to meet the guidance counselor, too.
3. **Volunteer** at your child's school. With cutbacks in education, parent volunteers are more important than ever and the wealth of extracurricular activities at most middle schools offer a terrific opportunity to get involved. For example, you might become an assistant coach, a guest speaker, or a chaperone for special outings and events; you can help with fundraisers, school mailings, and other organizational tasks. Think about your areas of expertise and how you might be of service to your teen's school, and watch for volunteer opportunities in school flyers and announcements. As a volunteer, you'll get a closer look at what goes on in school, and you'll set a wonderful example for your teen by providing an important community service.

4. **Join the parent organization** at your child's school (the Parent-Teacher Association (PTA), Parent-Teacher Organization (PTO), Parent Club, or other variation). These organizations promote communication between the school and home, keeping parents informed about school issues and giving parents a say in what's happening at the school. They often sponsor fundraisers that can help bring positive activities or amenities (such as books, sports equipment, and computers) to your teen's school.

You're the Most Powerful Influence

"Kids who learn from their parents or caregivers about the risks of drugs are 36 percent less likely to smoke marijuana than kids who don't. Fifty percent less likely to use inhalants. Fifty-six percent less likely to use LSD. Still think there's not much you can say or do? You are the most powerful influence in your child's daily life."

—BARRY MCCAFFREY,
DIRECTOR OF THE OFFICE OF NATIONAL DRUG CONTROL POLICY

Being Involved at Home

While it's important to be involved at school, your biggest impact will come from your involvement at home. To give your teen the support he needs during this year of academic challenges and physical and intellectual changes:

1. **Make education a priority at home.** Establish clear guidelines for when and where homework should be done and make sure homework takes precedence over other activities. Provide a supportive learning environment at home and create a comfortable and personalized study area for your child.

2. **Talk with your teen.** Ask questions and let your teen know that you care about what's going on. Avoid preaching to and judging; instead, speak honestly and openly about your emotions and your concerns, and be sure to talk to your teen about impor-

tant issues such as drugs, sex, and violence. (Remember, if you don't talk to your teen about these matters, someone else will.)

3. **Listen to your teen.** When your teen talks, make sure you listen. We convey more through tone than through the actual words we use. If you're not listening carefully, you may miss out on the signals your teen is trying to send you—and the signal you'll send your teen is that you don't really care about what she has to say. As you listen, paraphrase what your teen is saying to be sure you understand your teen correctly, and always acknowledge how your teen feels. Even if you think your teen is being overly emotional and immature (he is, after all, still only an adolescent), it's important to recognize that his feelings are real. If you tell him he shouldn't be feeling a certain way, he might not be willing to share his feelings with you in the future.

4. **Model good behavior.** Be a good role model for your teen. Act morally and responsibly; demonstrate trustworthiness, fairness, and reliability; and always treat others, especially your teen, with respect. Your teen can learn by your example. She is not likely to appreciate being punished for showing up late to school if you are always late for work. Actions will speak louder than words when your teen is growing into adulthood.

PAST, PRESENT, AND FUTURE

YOUR teen has a wonderful, exciting year ahead—a year full of changes and challenges that will help him become a more complete person. Physically, he will develop a new body; intellectually, he will develop important reasoning and problem-solving skills; emotionally, he will develop an independent identity as he forms close relationships with his peers; and academically, he will be asked to think about things and express himself in increasingly sophisticated ways.

It will be a wonderful year, but it may often be a difficult year for both of you as your relationship with your child changes as she strives for more and more independence. Childhood is now in the past, adulthood is still yet to come, and your teen is very much in the middle of things during this important transitional year. Rachael Dudzic, now a senior in high school, expressed the challenges of navigating this emotional middle ground in "Those Days, Now These," a beautiful poem written for her eighth grade English class at St. Stephen School in Oil City, Pennsylvania:

THOSE DAYS, **NOW THESE**
Rachael Dudzic, 1997

Clouds of crying and tears
Sunrays of smiles and laughter
Days full of dancing and joy

Clouds of emotion and feelings,
Sunrays of fun and friends,
Days full of decisions and problems
Everyone has to grow up

Tables covered with puzzles,
Boxes crammed with toys
Rooms full of fun and delight

Tables covered with books
Boxes crammed full of papers
Rooms full of anxiety and pressure
Everyone has to learn sometime

Pictures of children at play
Portraits done by miniature fingers and hands
Memories of wishing to reach the third shelf

Pictures of growing adults at work
Portraits by experienced, capable hands
Memories of wishing to capture the moon,
Everyone has to grow taller

Life was so simple when your dad was your hero,
Life was so easy when everyone loved you.
Now, life seems hard when your dad is just your parent,
And life is so tough when love has to be earned.

Author's Note

Use this book in the way that it will help you most. You can read straight through, chapter by chapter, or you can skip ahead to the chapters that will help you with your most pressing concerns at the moment, such as your teen's social development or standardized tests. As you read, remember that the parent-child relationship is a dynamic one, changing as both you and your child grow older and learn more about each other and yourselves. Think positive, stay involved, and remember that you are still your child's most important teacher.

chapter 2

What Your 8th Grader Is Learning in School

FROM APPROXIMATELY 7:30 A.M. to 2:30 P.M., Monday through Friday, your teen is in school. Just how does he spend those seven hours? What goes on in the classroom? What is he learning, and how can you help ensure that he learns well?

There are many strategies you can use to help your child do well academically, and we'll discuss those tactics in detail in Chapter 4. But before you decide which strategies to use, you must first understand the curriculum that's been designed for your eighth grader. What will your child be studying? What is he expected to learn in each class?

Eighth grade is a very important year academically. In most states, eighth graders will take standardized tests in reading and math (and increasingly in writing, social studies, and science as well) to see how they and their schools measure up against state achievement standards. In addition, in most school systems, eighth graders need to be adequately prepared for high school, so much of their work this year will focus on building the knowledge and skills they'll need to succeed at that level. And eighth grade is also a year in which teens reach an important new level of intellectual development.

The typical eighth grader is entering what child psychologist Jean Piaget (1896–1980) called the "formal operational" stage of intellectual development. In this stage, which typically begins around the onset of puberty, children develop the ability to think abstractly and reason hypothetically. When presented with a problem, eighth graders should be able to formulate hypotheses about possible causes and systematically test those hypotheses, and they should be able to test possible solutions through the same hypothetical reasoning process.

Education Terms

Your child's **curriculum** includes the ideas, facts, processes, and skills (academic, physical, and social) that educators and specialists have deemed important for your child to learn in this grade. The aim of national and statewide **standards** is to provide guideposts or checkpoints to help parents and educators ensure that students are on track for mastering the ideas, facts, processes, and skills for their grade level.

The development of these skills helps explain why many adolescents seem to suddenly be so argumentative—they're testing out their newfound reasoning and problem-solving skills. It also helps explain why a fifth grader will have difficulty understanding that his actions today will have an effect on his future while an eighth grader should be able to see some connection between the past, present, and future and imagine possible future outcomes.

The way that your adolescent thinks about and understands the world is therefore changing, and her courses will help her with this development by challenging her to think in different ways. Her science classes will focus on the scientific method, for example, and she'll be asked to perform symbolic operations in math (algebra). In English and social studies classes, she'll use characters and historical events to explore abstract ideas such as justice, freedom, and equality, and she'll be expected to develop and support logical arguments.

THE 8TH GRADE SCHOOL SCHEDULE

THE typical middle school day starts between 7:30–8:30 A.M. and ends between 2:30–3:30 P.M. Those hours are usually divided into seven to nine 45- to 60-minute periods. Typically, students will attend their "core four" courses—English, math, social studies, and science—one period each day for the entire year while they attend other courses on a rotating schedule, switching subjects each marking period or alternating subjects on different days of the week. Thus, while your child may have English every day first period for the whole school year, her second period class may be community service for the first and third marking periods, business for the second marking period, and speech for the fourth marking period. Or, your eighth grader's fourth period class may be computers Wednesdays and Fridays and foreign language Mondays, Tuesdays, and Thursdays.

Alternatively, your teen's school may use "block scheduling": two periods scheduled back-to-back to allow for interdisciplinary approaches to the subject matter. For example, science *and* math may be scheduled for the first block of the day (the first 90 minutes) while English *and* social studies will occupy the second block (the second 90 minutes). Some middle schools even use block scheduling for the entire day, creating a four period day, for example, instead of eight. In this case, even the core four courses become rotating subjects.

Block scheduling allows teachers more flexibility in how they use their time, giving them the opportunity to explore topics in greater detail and make strong connections across the curriculum. The first period math and science teachers, for example, may decide to spend the entire period working on a math concept (without covering any science) and the next day spend the entire 90 minutes on a science project which incorporates that math skill. During the English/social studies block, students may spend two consecutive periods reading slave narratives and discussing the social and economic effects of slavery.

With or without block scheduling, eighth grade teachers typically work in teams to develop interdisciplinary approaches to the material. Students can therefore look at ideas and information from different perspectives and see how they are relevant in many different ways. With a topic such as genetics, for example, teachers can make connections across the curriculum, with lessons in heredity, probability, ethics, and literature (such as a science fiction story about genetic engineering).

There are as many variations in schedules as there are middle schools, but most eighth graders will have a schedule similar to one of the following sample schedules:

7-Period Day, No Block Scheduling

Time	Monday	Tuesday	Wednesday	Thursday	Friday
7:45–8:00	Homeroom	Homeroom	Homeroom	Homeroom	Homeroom
8:03–8:53	Art	Music	Art	Music	Art
8:56–9:46	English	English	English	English	English
9:49–10:39	Phys Ed	Health	Phys Ed	Health	Phys Ed
10:42–11:32	Math	Math	Math	Math	Math
11:35–12:25	Science	Science	Science	Science	Science
12:28–12:59	Lunch	Lunch	Lunch	Lunch	Lunch
1:02–1:52	Social Studies	Social Studies	Social Studies	Social Studies	Social Studies
1:55–2:45	Spanish	Computers	Spanish	Computers	Spanish

Modified Block Schedule (6 periods)

Time	Monday	Tuesday	Wednesday	Thursday	Friday
8:00–9:30	Science & Math	Science & Math	Science & Math	Science & Math	Science & Math
9:35–10:20	Intermediate French	Intermediate French	Intermediate French	Intermediate French	Intermediate French
10:25–11:55	English & Social Studies	English & Social Studies	English & Social Studies	English & Social Studies	English & Social Studies
12:00–12:35	Lunch	Lunch	Lunch	Lunch	Lunch
12:40–1:25	Phys Ed	Phys Ed	Phys Ed	Phys Ed	Phys Ed
1:30–2:15	Art Elective: Photography	Clubs/ Study Hall	Art Elective: Photography	Clubs/ Study Hall	Art Elective: Photography
2:20–3:05	Free Elective I: Community Service	Free Elective II: Journalism	Free Elective I: Community Service	Free Elective II: Journalism	Free Elective I: Community Service

These schedules represent an average student in an average school. Your child's schedule and class load may vary from these representative schedules.

THE 8TH GRADE CURRICULUM

WHILE there is a movement to create national educational standards, the power to determine curriculum remains with states and individual schools. Each state establishes a set of standards (learning goals) for each grade level, and each school then develops a curriculum to meet those learning objectives and address the specific needs of its students and community. Thus, while your state may require all eighth graders to learn the history of the United States through World War II, *how* students learn that history will be determined by each individual school.

While each state has its own standards and each school has a unique curriculum, most eighth grade programs are actually very similar in terms of the specific skills and knowledge eighth graders are expected to learn. The rest of this chapter outlines the typical eighth grade curriculum. Your teen's exact curriculum may vary from this outline, so it is important to request a copy of the complete curriculum from your teen's school. Your state standards should be available on the state's website, and your school may also have copies of those standards for distribution to parents.

English

In elementary school, your child spent a significant portion of her school day learning how to read and write. By the fourth or fifth grade, your child made the leap from "learning to read" to "reading to learn." Since then, your child's reading lessons have been focusing on *understanding* what he reads. And he'll be reading and writing more sophisticated material than ever before.

Reading/Literature

Your eighth grader will be expected to do a significant amount of reading outside of the classroom. He will read a variety of texts from a range of genres, including stories, novels, essays, poems, and plays, and he may be asked to keep a weekly journal in which he records his reactions to and questions about the texts that he reads. A typical text might be *To Kill a Mockingbird* by Harper Lee or *The House on Mango Street* by Sandra Cisneros—coming of age stories in which the characters face issues and make decisions that help determine who they are and what they believe in. Typically, texts are thematically based and complement subjects being taught in other classes. Thus, while eighth graders are studying Native Americans and Westward Expansion in their social studies class, they'll read literature written by and about Native Americans, such as N. Scott Momaday's *The Way to Rainy Mountain*.

As they read and discuss these texts, eighth graders will be expected to develop skills in four specific areas:

Word Power

Your eighth grader will continue to expand her vocabulary with increasingly sophisticated words. Below is a sampling of the words she will learn:

adage	banter	cryptic	dexterous	enmity	frugal
gaunt	haughty	impunity	judicious	kindred	longevity
myriad	nonentity	ostracize	prodigious	qualm	renown
scapegoat	tenet	voracious			

1. **Increased Word Knowledge.** Your teen will continue formal vocabulary building through weekly word lists and an examination of word roots, suffixes, and prefixes. She will also learn how to approximate meaning by using word root and suffix/prefix clues. In addition, eighth graders learn how to use context to determine the correct meaning of a word when the dictionary offers multiple meanings and how to determine the approximate meaning of a word without a dictionary by using context.

2. **Understanding of Increasingly Complex Texts.** Your eighth grader will be reading more complex materials this year—texts that use more sophisticated vocabulary and sentence structure, deal with more sophisticated ideas and abstractions, and require readers to draw more of their own conclusions based upon "clues" in the text. Students will learn how to summarize these texts, identify and express the main idea of a passage, and identify the sequence of events in a story or article. They will also spend a significant amount of time developing reasoning skills by learning how to use specific details from the text to support an argument.

3. **Recognition of Elements of Literature and Literary Devices.** The literature eighth graders will read will be more sophisticated, so it will require a better understanding of literature to grasp meaning. Eighth graders will build on their knowledge of the elements of literature—plot, setting, characterization,

point of view, tone, symbolism, style, and theme—and learn to recognize them in increasingly complex literature.

They will also learn to recognize more sophisticated literary devices, such as allusion, complex rhyme schemes, and satire while reinforcing knowledge of devices such as alliteration and figurative language.

4. **Literary Analysis.** By reading carefully and recognizing elements of literature and writing strategies, students should be able to conduct basic literary analysis to determine theme. They will be encouraged to make connections to their own lives and to historical and current situations. They will learn how to identify cause and effect relationships in a text, to predict possible outcomes of a reading situation, to compare and contrast similar aspects (such as character or conflict) within a text or between two or more texts.

Eighth grade has been much more of a "pre-high school" experience for my son than earlier in middle school. The demands on the kids to really learn to research and write independently, and to hone their study skills are much higher than in 7th grade. As much as curriculum, they are learning the skills they will need to do well in High School.

—A PARENT FROM WESTCHESTER, NEW YORK

Writing/Composition

This year there will be a continued emphasis on writing as a *process.* Your eighth grader's writing instruction will focus on the five steps that create a final written product: pre-writing or "brainstorming" strategies, such as listing, freewriting, mapping/diagramming, and outlining; drafting; reviewing; revising; and editing.

In many classes, your teen will be expected to participate in peer reviews. She will share her writing with her classmates, who will give her feedback on her work. At the same time, she will be giving her classmates feedback as well. Thus, she will be developing two very important skills: the ability to judge the effectiveness of a piece of writing and to accept constructive criticism from her peers. She will then be expected to use her own evaluation and the evaluation of her peers to make appropriate revisions to her work.

Your teen will develop these evaluation skills through lessons that focus on several specific writing strategies. In the eighth grade, there will be a strong emphasis on understanding audience and purpose and on organizing ideas effectively. Your teen may therefore practice several different ways of organizing ideas, such as order of importance, comparison and contrast, and cause and effect. He will also learn strategies for writing more meaningful introductions and conclusions, and because your teen's argumentation and abstract thinking skills are developing, he will see an increased emphasis on stating a clear thesis and providing detailed support for that thesis.

Eighth graders will write several types of essays and stories, with most papers running five to seven paragraphs in length. In a **narrative** essay, students will tell a story based on their own observation or experience or from their own imagination. They will be expected to use a great deal of description and dialogue to help readers "see" and "hear" what happened. They will also write several **expository** essays that explain a concept or **argumentative** essays that state and support a position. For example, your teen might write an essay explaining the difference between two characters or argue why the school should or should not implement a uniform dress code. Finally, eighth graders typically spend a considerable amount of time in the library conducting research for a **research paper**. They will formulate a research question, seek appropriate sources, assess those sources, and incorporate supporting material into a research report.

In all of these essays, the emphasis will be on the *idea* your eighth grader is "arguing," and on providing strong support for that argument. Your child will also be learning how to logically organize and develop his ideas and how to write in a way that demonstrates an understanding of his audience, such as selecting an appropriate style and tone. And a good deal of attention will be paid to helping your teen develop a strong writing voice so that his personality comes across in his writing.

On the sentence level, your writer will be expected to pay greater attention to word choice (for example, using "devastated" instead of "very upset" or "teeming" instead of "really full") and to use several stylistic and poetic devices in her work, including alliteration, figurative language (similes and metaphors), and personification. He will be expected to have greater variety in sentence structure and to be able to edit his work carefully to eliminate grammatical errors.

Your teen's English teacher will likely provide him with a rubric (a detailed scoring guide used to evaluate subjective assignments such as essays) that clearly states the expectations for his essays. This rubric will help him understand how his work will be assessed and help him develop criteria for evaluating his own work. The following two pages show you a sample rubric that a teacher would use to grade a writing sample.

Grammar

Eighth grade grammar instruction will help students write in complete sentences, eliminating sentence fragments and run-ons from their writing. In class, they will study more complex grammatical structures, including various phrases and clauses, and will therefore be expected to write increasingly complex sentences and use various sentence-combining techniques. Your teen should be able to recognize and correctly use the parts of speech, and he will see an emphasis on proper punctuation, such as when to use a semi-colon instead of a comma and the various rules for comma use. These lessons will typically be taught as part of the writing process, using sentences from student essays as examples.

Category:	Knowledge and Understanding	Organization	Use of Support Material	Sentence Structure	Vocabulary	Grammar
5.0	Your child exhibits understanding and interpretation of the task.	Your child develops ideas with a coherent, logical, and orderly approach.	Your child exhibits use of relevant and accurate examples to support ideas.	Your child uses varied sentence structure.	Your child uses effective language and challenging vocabulary.	Your child conventional spelling, punctuation, paragraphing, capitalization, grammar, and usage.
4.0	Your child has a good understanding of the topic and writes about it in an imaginative and creative way.	Your child has organized and developed his/her ideas in a coherent and well-defined manner.	Your child purposely uses support material from the story that is relevant and appropriate.	Your child shows the ability to vary sentence structure.	Your child uses sophisticated vocabulary.	Your child makes few mechanical errors, if if any.
3.0	Your child shows an understanding of the topic and writes about it in a logical, practical way.	Your child had an obvious plan to develop his/her ideas that was satisfactory.	Your child has used some support material in an organized form.	Your child has used correct sentence structure, but there is little sentence variety.	Your child shows an average range of vocabulary.	Your child makes some mechanical errors, but they do not interfere with communication.

Category:	Knowledge and Understanding	Organization	Use of Support Material	Sentence Structure	Vocabulary	Grammar
2.0	Your child tries to develop the topic but digresses and writes about other topics as well.	Your child shows little organization and development of content.	Your child does not use relevant support material from the narrative.	Your child shows some knowledge of sentence structure but also writes in fragments or run-on sentences.	Your child uses inaccurate, inexact or vague language.	Your child makes many mechanical errors that interfere with communication.
1.0	Your child only addresses the topic minimally.	Your child shows no ability to organize or develop ideas.	Your child has not included or organized support material.	Your child does not have a sense of structure.	Your child uses inexact or immature language.	Your child makes mechanical errors that make the paper impossible to understand.
0.0	A ZERO paper would be one that shows no relation to the topic, is illegible, incoherent, or blank.	A ZERO paper would be one that shows no relation to the topic, is illegible, incoherent, or blank.	A ZERO paper would be one that shows no relation to the topic, is illegible, incoherent, or blank.	A ZERO paper would be one that shows no relation to the topic, is illegible, incoherent, or blank.	A ZERO paper would be one that shows no relation to the topic, is illegible, incoherent, or blank.	A ZERO paper would be one that shows no relation to the topic, is illegible, incoherent, or blank.

The Times They Are A-Changing

The middle school curriculum has been receiving a great deal of attention in the last few decades, and research findings and the influence of *Turning Points: Preparing American Youth for the 21st Century,* a remarkable guide to middle school reform, have resulted in several significant trends in middle school education:

1. **Character education.** Many schools are now implementing a formal curriculum in character education. One of the most common curricula is "Character Counts," a program developed by the Character Counts coalition of schools and organizations. The "Character Counts" curriculum teaches students about the following six "pillars" of good character:

trustworthiness	respect	responsibility
fairness	caring	citizenship

2. **Community service.** More and more emphasis is being placed on community service, which may be offered as an elective course or incorporated as a requirement in a social studies class.

3. **Increased interdisciplinary education.** Middle school educators are working to increase the number of interdisciplinary units in the curriculum, making more connections between content areas.

4. **Focus on health and fitness.** Physical education classes are moving away from an emphasis on sports and skills and toward a focus on general health and fitness. More and more middle schools are building their own fitness centers for students to work out after school and maintain physical health.

Math

In the Clinton Administration's Goals 2000 education initiative, eighth grade math was listed as one of the Department of Education's seven priorities. Specifically, the Department's goal is for all students to "master challenging mathematics, including the foundations of algebra and geometry, by the end of eighth grade." Your teen's curriculum will aim to achieve this goal by reinforcing old skills and teaching several important new math concepts in a way that emphasizes real-life uses of mathematics.

The typical eighth grade math curriculum will begin with a review of previously learned concepts, including:

➤ whole numbers and operations
➤ decimals
➤ fractions
➤ percentages
➤ translating word problems into expressions and solvable equations

Then, your teen will learn the following new math skills:

Basic probability and statistics
➤ How probability is calculated
➤ What probabilities are used for
➤ How statistical analyses can give us meaningful information
➤ How to calculate and use mean, median, and mode measurements
➤ How and why to use the function of standard deviation

Graphics
➤ How to interpret graphical information
➤ How to create visual representations of data in tables, charts and graphs

Algebra

➤ How to use variables and equations as problem-solving techniques

➤ How to add, subtract, and multiply polynomals

➤ How to graph and solve quadratic equations

Geometry

➤ How to classify and measure angles

➤ How to understand and use if-then statements and truth tables to determine logically equivalent statements

➤ How to use deductive and inductive reasoning techniques

➤ How to plan and write proofs

➤ How to use formulas to determine area and volume of geometric shapes

➤ How to use length and areas to solve geometric problems

➤ How to find and use ratios and proportions

➤ How to define basic tangent, sine, and cosine ratios

➤ The Pythagorean theorem and its applications

When possible, these subjects (such as graphics) will often incorporate use of computer technology.

Science

For several years now, your child has been "doing" science, learning some basic scientific facts and, in recent years, learning to use the scientific method to investigate the natural world. The eighth grade science curriculum covers disciplines your child has already explored in previous years: earth science, life sciences, and physical science. This year, however, your teen will go deeper into each subject, learning some of the principles that underlie the scientific facts he has been learning over the years. For example, your child should already know that matter is made of atoms and molecules; now he will learn the structure of those atoms and molecules and the laws of their interaction. As your child is learning increasingly complicated material, he will be conducting experiments to test some of the principles he learns. In fact, the eighth grade science curriculum is highly exploratory in nature, and much of the learning takes place through hands-on experimentation.

This is a crucial year for scientific investigation, for the scientific principles that your eighth grader learns lay the foundation for more advanced work in high school. Because your eighth grader is developing more systematic approaches to problems, and because much work is lab-based, he will need to understand and apply the **scientific method** to test these principles. Your teen will usually follow experiment procedures from a textbook or lab manual, but on occasion your child will be challenged to come up with experimental procedures himself to test his hypotheses. He will be expected to write up the results of his experiments in detailed lab reports that include text and graphics, and he will be expected to understand and follow proper lab procedures.

The Scientific Method:

❐ Identify or state the problem
❐ Formulate a hypothesis
❐ Develop experimental procedures
❐ Conduct an experiment
❐ Gather and record data
❐ Analyze and interpret data
❐ Draw conclusions

Physical Science

The typical eighth grade curriculum covers the following areas of physical science:

➤ **Chemical concepts:** different types of chemical reactions and the properties of acids and bases.
➤ **The structure of matter:** the structure of atoms and molecules.
➤ **The laws governing the behavior of matter:** force, motion, work, and simple mechanics.

Life Sciences

Your child will learn:

> ➤ the basic biology of living organisms: cells, structures, systems (some classes may include the dissection of animals)
> ➤ the principles of genetics, heredity, and bioengineering
> ➤ the system of classification of organisms

Earth Science

Your teen will learn:

> ➤ basic geology (geological eras, plate tectonics)
> ➤ the theory of evolution
> ➤ the system of classification of plants
> ➤ principles of organic systems and interactions (ecosystems)

Social Studies

Eighth grade social studies classes (which may be called "U.S. History") typically focus on two main topics: the history of the United States from colonization to the 20th century (usually through World War II) and civics: what it means to be a citizen of the United States. The course will emphasize an understanding of cause and effect in history and seeing history as a way of understanding the present and shaping the future. Most eighth graders will conduct a social studies research project that may include primary research. Students may, for example, conduct their own interviews to create a history of a local area or of their family. In this class, students also learn to take an active role in political systems by forming a mock senate, for example, or conducting a mock trial. If there is no separate community service class, students will also often conduct local or national service projects as part of this course.

History of the United States

Throughout the year, this course will cover the major events, persons, and themes in American history, including:

> ➤ colonization
> ➤ American Revolution

> the development of Constitution and Amendments
> Westward expansion
> slavery
> the Civil War
> Reconstruction
> immigration
> industrialization
> World War I
> the Depression
> World War II

These historical events are related to current issues and events, helping students to connect the present to the past in a meaningful way and allowing students to make extrapolations about the future.

Most classes will use a combination of textbooks and primary sources to allow students to see history from several different points of view. For example, they may read slave narratives, examine materials from a slave auction, and read speeches by abolitionists and newspaper accounts in addition to the material in their textbook. Students will also be expected to master the geography of the United States at various times in its history.

Democratic Principles

Students will also learn democratic principles by carefully studying the U.S. Constitution and its Amendments, particularly the Bill of Rights. Your teen will learn what these documents are, what they mean, and how they affect us in our real lives. Specifically, he will learn:

> the tenets of democracy
> the evolution of democratic principles
> the democratic process
> the basics of the United States legal system

To help students understand how to be effective citizens in a democracy, many social studies classes emphasize debate and spend considerable time helping students learn to distinguish between fact and opinion.

While most eighth grade social studies curricula focus on U.S. history, some states require eighth graders to learn world history instead, reserving U.S. history for another grade. A typical world history curriculum will cover the major events (wars, revolutions, inventions, achievements) in world history to impart an understanding of the various ways societies have governed themselves over time and how the structure of a society reflects its values. Students will examine various conflicts, their causes, and how societies dealt with those conflicts; how societies have produced, distributed, and consumed goods; how politics, economics, and culture have been affected by technology; and how societies have affected and been affected by their environment.

Class Size Matters

"Reducing class size is one of the most important investments we can make in our children's future," said former President Bill Clinton. As a result, in 1999 Congress approved a $1.2 billion payment toward the president's effort to hire teachers and expand school buildings to reduce the teacher-student ratio. In 2000, an additional $450 million was offered so that a total of nearly 50,000 teachers could be hired through the Federal Class-Size Reduction Program. Inspired by federal support, almost half the states in the union have made an effort to reduce class size, and therefore to improve the quality of education. As a testament to its success, schools that were able to hire more teachers with Class-Size Reduction funds have reduced the average number of students in each classroom from 23 students to 18 students.

SOURCE: "THE CLASS-SIZE REDUCTION REPORT,"
U.S. DEPARTMENT OF EDUCATION, SEPTEMBER 2000.

Rotating Subjects

Two to four of the periods in your eighth grader's school day are typically filled by **rotating subjects**: required courses in the curriculum outside of the core four. These rotating subjects often include important courses in foreign languages, art and music, computers, library, and physical education.

Foreign Languages

While some schools offer foreign languages as electives, most eighth graders are required to begin study of a foreign language or to continue studies begun in previous grades, and in some states all students are required to study language five days a week. Foreign language study is required for high school graduation as well as admission to most colleges. Spanish and French remain the two most common middle school language offerings, though many schools also offer German, Italian, and Latin. Your child may be required to take short introductory courses in each language offered at her school or to choose one language for focused study.

Foreign language studies will provide students with a basic knowledge of grammar for speaking, listening, and writing, as well as an understanding of the cultures in which that language is spoken. In an introductory Spanish course, for example, your eighth grader will learn basic present tense verb conjugations, pronouns, and everyday vocabulary words and phrases. She will learn the rules for word order in a Spanish sentence and everyday expressions. She will also learn about Latin American customs, holidays, and foods, and she will learn the basic geography of Spanish-speaking countries throughout the world. While she will learn to read and write basic sentences in the language, her courses will focus on conversation skills.

Art and Music

The art and music classes available to your eighth grader will depend upon the art and music curriculum offered in previous grades and upon the art and music resources available to the middle school. In a typical eighth grade art class, your child may be expected to:

➤ understand and produce the elements of art: line, shape, color, texture, space
➤ use the elements of art to convey emotion
➤ interpret emotion in a work of art

➤ understand characteristics of several artistic media
➤ use several different media to create works of art
➤ gain an understanding of other cultures through an examination of their artwork

This type of art class provides a general or overview approach that exposes students to a variety of genres and media. But your eighth grader's school may require an art class that focuses on one particular art form, such as drawing, painting, ceramics, or photography. (In many cases, schools will provide a general art course as a required rotating subject and include a course in a specific genre, such as photography, as an elective.)

An eighth grade music class will typically have one of three focuses:

1. the historical development of music and how music is affected by history and geography
2. reading and writing music
3. performing music (in chorus, orchestra, and/or band)

As with foreign languages, your child's school may require students to study all three areas on a rotating basis, or your child may be allowed to choose the musical area to study.

Physical Education/Health

Physical education remains an important part of your child's curriculum, and your teen's curriculum will probably include several physical education sessions each week. These sessions are a much-needed outlet for your teen's energy, which is running high during this period of dramatic physical change. And of course your child no longer has recess, so physical education class is the only chance he will get to be physically active during the school day.

The goals of eighth grade physical education are threefold:

1. **To continue to build students' self-esteem** through development of individual skill in team and individual sports. Your child has left behind most of the games played in elementary

school and has moved into organized sporting events with specific rules and strategies. These team and individual sports typically include (depending upon facilities and equipment): soccer, basketball, swimming, hockey, baseball, softball, volleyball, gymnastics, tennis, and track and field activities. Even if a teen is not particularly athletic, he will have the opportunity to improve his speed in the 50-yard dash, for example, or develop a more powerful tennis serve through these activities.

2. **To continue to build sportsmanship and teamwork skills**, including leadership, cooperation, fairness, and courtesy. To develop these skills, students may be asked to serve in various positions throughout the school year, such as team captain, referee, equipment manager, timer, and scorekeeper. Your teen will be expected to understand the rules and strategies for the sports in which she participates.

3. **To continue to improve students' physical fitness:** strength, endurance, flexibility, power, speed, and agility. This goal is receiving greater emphasis in many schools as the focus shifts from sports and skills to physical fitness. Students may be spending significantly more time weight training and jogging around the track and less time practicing a specific sport.

Your teen's fitness may be tested against the Presidential Fitness Program, which was developed over thirty years ago to encourage healthy lifestyles and physical fitness achievement in children and teens. For eighth graders, the Presidential Fitness Program includes activities with which your teen should be very familiar, for she has probably been tested in these same activities (with some variation) since elementary school:

➤ **Sit and Reach:** Tests flexibility of hamstring and lower back muscles by measuring how far students reach forward in a sitting position.

➤ **Curl-Ups (Sit-Ups):** Tests strength and endurance of abdominal muscles by measuring the number of curl-ups performed in one minute.

➤ **Push-Ups:** Tests upper arm strength and endurance by measuring the number of push-ups completed. (In elementary school, upper arm strength was probably measured by pull-ups rather than push-ups.)

➤ **Mile Run/Walk:** Tests cardiovascular endurance by measuring time to complete a mile run or walk.

➤ **Shuttle Run:** Tests speed and endurance by measuring time to complete the shuttle run.

Boys Presidential Fitness Test Standards:

Fitness Test Item	Age 12	Age 13	Age 14
V-Sit and Reach (inches)	+4.0	+3.5	+4.5
Curl-Ups (number of)	50	53	56
Push-Ups (number of)	31	39	40
Mile Run/Walk (min:sec)	7:11	6:50	6:26
Shuttle Run (seconds)	9.8	9.5	9.1

Girls Presidential Fitness Test Standards:

Fitness Test Item	Age 12	Age 13	Age 14
V-Sit and Reach (inches)	+7.0	+7.0	+8.0
Curl-Ups (number of)	45	46	47
Push-Ups (number of)	20	21	20
Mile Run/Walk (min:sec)	8:20	8:13	8:59
Shuttle Run (seconds)	10.4	10.2	10.1

(For more information about the President's Challenge Physical Fitness Program, see the program website at www.fitness.gov., or visit www.indiana.edu/~preschal/.)

In addition, many eighth grade curricula include health classes that alternate with the physical education classes. In the typical health class, students learn about body wellness by studying physical fitness concepts and nutrition. Specific topics may include:

➤ the body systems: skeletal, muscular, and circulatory
➤ the types and benefits of exercise
➤ the components of fitness
➤ sport safety
➤ sport injuries
➤ first aid procedures
➤ proper nutrition
➤ hygiene

Computer/Educational Technology

Many schools now include a computer or educational technology course as a required part of the eighth grade curriculum. The typical computer course will teach your child:

➤ the basics of computer hardware
➤ word processing skills, including basic document design
➤ basic desktop publishing (computer graphics)
➤ keyboarding using the "home row" to achieve both typing speed and accuracy
➤ how to prepare a basic spreadsheet
➤ how to browse and conduct basic research on the Internet
➤ how to prepare a presentation using Microsoft PowerPoint

What your teen learns here will often be reinforced across the curriculum. For example, students may use spreadsheets in science class to calculate the results of an experiment and then present those results in a PowerPoint presentation.

Library

Your middle schooler may still be attending required library sessions, and, like computer education, these skills will be reinforced across the curriculum. In library (or "media center" or "resource room") sessions, your teen will learn more advanced research skills. She will be expected to know how to find and evaluate sources, and she will be expected to be able to find information through a variety of sources, including encyclopedias, periodicals, books, and the Internet. She will also be expected to know how to cite her reference materials. These sessions will usually be tied to specific projects in other classes, such as a research project on Industrialization for English and social studies.

Electives

Eighth graders will often have the opportunity to choose elective courses beyond their core four and rotating subjects. Electives are often set up like the rotating subjects so that students can experience three or four electives throughout the school year. These electives are an important part of the eighth grade curriculum, for they offer your teen a chance to explore new subjects and to delve deeper into current hobbies and interests.

Elective offerings vary widely from school to school. In some schools, foreign language and computer courses are required rotating subjects while other schools will offer these courses as electives, saving the requirement for high school. Below is a list of some of the more common elective offerings (please note that it is unlikely that any one middle school will have *all* of these subjects):

➤ art (including specific media or genres)
➤ band
➤ business/entrepreneurship
➤ chorus
➤ community service
➤ dance
➤ drama
➤ foreign language
➤ home and careers
➤ journalism
➤ keyboarding/typing

➤ orchestra
➤ speech
➤ video production
➤ work experience
➤ yearbook

On occasion, middle schools may also offer electives in specific subject areas. Some schools, for example, offer special electives such as the following:

➤ **literature electives** in science fiction, Shakespeare, or literature and film
➤ **science electives** in subjects like genetics, marine science, or astronomy
➤ **social studies electives** in campaign and election issues or Native American history
➤ **technology electives** in computer programming, game theory, or graphic design

Study Skills

To handle this challenging schedule and curriculum, your eighth grader will need to have a good handle on her study skills. By the eighth grade, your teen should be able to:

➤ **manage time** effectively by creating and following a schedule for completing work
➤ **take effective notes** by differentiating between main and supporting ideas, between key facts and specific examples and details
➤ **manage projects** by breaking them down into manageable tasks
➤ **solve problems** effectively and creatively by correctly identifying the problem, brainstorming solutions, evaluating the possible solutions, and assessing the success of the chosen solution

These skills are not an official part of the curriculum—that is, they probably won't be specifically taught in any class—but they will be reinforced across the curriculum. Problem-solving skills, for example, will be steadily built in math and science units. Teachers will often help with project management skills by giving students specific deadlines for the components of a project.

If your teen has difficulty in any of these areas, she may be able to get extra support from the guidance office.

Trouble Ahead?

Because eighth grade, in most school systems, is the last year before high school, students really need to brush up their academic skills. Your eighth grader may be headed for trouble in high school if:

❒ She doesn't know how to use a computer for research and word processing.

❒ She can't handle homework without help, or she won't do homework without your encouragement or insistence.

❒ She doesn't communicate well with her teachers.

❒ She doesn't know how to take effective notes or manage time.

❒ She has difficulty expressing herself orally and/or in writing.

SUMMARY

AS you can see, eighth grade is a unique, transitional year for your adolescent, whose curriculum will challenge him to use his developing reasoning skills and give him opportunities to explore areas of interest through elective courses and rotating subjects. His curriculum will be highly interdisciplinary, so skills and subject matter will be reinforced in several classes throughout the year. It is important for your teen to manage time well and develop and maintain strong study skills. Don't be surprised if he experiences some growing pains this year as he faces new, more difficult subject matter and approaches; he may need a little more time to develop his abstract thinking skills and may need extra support as he learns how to approach problems systematically. You can help your teen through these difficult times and stay involved throughout the school year by following the suggestions in Chapter 4.

chapter 3

Extracurricular Activities

IN ADDITION to working through the challenging curriculum of eighth grade, your teen will likely be engaged in (or at least interested in) one or more extracurricular activities. As you may recall from your middle school years, extracurricular activities are an important part of the eighth grade experience, enhancing social and intellectual development, as well as providing an important structured outlet for adolescent physical energy. In fact, many education experts believe that activities outside the classroom are *as important* to your teen's personal and academic growth as the activities that go on inside the classroom and that they are an essential part of the learning process. Indeed, many educators feel that the term "co-curricular" is more appropriate than "extracurricular" because of how much these activities build and reinforce the skills taught in the classroom.

WHAT ARE EXTRACURRICULAR ACTIVITIES, EXACTLY?

THE extracurricular activities at your child's school are those activities that are offered outside of (or in addition to) the normal academic curriculum. Because they are sponsored by the school, these extracurricular activities involve various members of the school community, bringing together faculty, staff, students, and parents. Faculty and staff may serve as club advisors, coaches, and chaperones for special events while parents often participate as assistant coaches, special guest speakers, chaperones, and fund raisers for club activities.

Middle school extracurricular activities usually include sports (both competitive and intramural) and clubs of all kinds, from academic clubs (such as the Math Team) to theater groups to clubs that explore and celebrate a particular culture. Clubs usually meet during a free period set aside specifically for extracurricular activities and/or after school. Competitive athletic teams will usually meet every day during the sport season (usually about three months long) while clubs typically meet once or twice a week all year long, with extra sessions in the weeks before a special production or performance date.

> Extracurricular activities are very important in developing the whole child. We want well-rounded individuals, and the first thing we tell students when they get here in sixth grade is to get involved. . . . For them, the social contact is important. They have a pretty rigorous academic day, and they need some time to enjoy their friends and explore their interests.
>
> —BARBARA LYON, 8TH GRADE GUIDANCE COUNSELOR
> TAYLOR ROAD MIDDLE SCHOOL, ALPHARETTA, GEORGIA

Your son or daughter's school will have a specific policy for participation in extracurricular activities. A typical middle school allows students to participate in any extracurricular activity so long as they do not fail more than one subject per marking period. Certain activities, such as competitive sports, may have additional eligibility requirements, and parents will be required to fill out a waiver or release form before their teen can participate on an interscholastic sports team. This form typically asks for contact and insurance information in the case of an emergency as well as any information, such as allergies or current medications, that may affect how your child is treated if hurt. The form also requires you to acknowledge that your teen will participate in an activity that carries the risk of physical injury and possibly even death. You may also be required to purchase insurance for your teen if he is not currently covered. Be sure to read this waiver carefully to understand the school's policies, procedures, and liabilities.

WHY SHOULD YOUR CHILD PARTICIPATE?

THE benefits of extracurricular activities are numerous and important. Study after study has shown that students who participate in extracurricular activities—particularly sports—have higher grade averages, fewer disciplinary problems, better attendance records, and a significantly lower chance of dropping out of school. They're also less likely to smoke, drink, or do drugs. Why? Because these activities help teens develop important social, academic, and physical skills. They also allow adolescents to pursue their own talents and interests, a critical factor in developing a strong sense of self. Here's a breakdown of some of the specific benefits of extracurricular activities:

Increased Knowledge and Tolerance

Extracurricular activities offer your child a chance to broaden her horizons by learning new ideas and skills and learning about new people and places. In a Diversity Club, for example, your teen might learn about Hindu customs or listen to music from Senegal. In the Young Entrepreneurs Club, your teen might learn how to develop an effective advertising campaign and how to use desktop publishing software to develop print advertisements.

Extracurricular Activity Consent Form

Student Name: _____ Date of Birth: _____

Home Phone: _____ Grade: _____

Mother's Name: _____ Employer: _____ Phone: _____

Father's Name: _____ Employer: _____ Phone: _____

If a parent or guardian cannot be located when my child is ill or injured, contact:

1. _____ Relationship: _____ Phone: _____

2. _____ Relationship: _____ Phone: _____

I/We authorize permission for medical treatment by: (circle) EMT   PHYSICIAN
I authorize transportation to a medical facility by: (circle) AMBULANCE   PHYSICIAN

My/Our student wishes to participate in the following activities: (Initial all that apply)

- _____ Academic Decathlon
- _____ Baseball
- _____ Basketball
- _____ Cheerleading
- _____ Football
- _____ Golf
- _____ Mat Maids
- _____ Music
- _____ Softball
- _____ Speech/Debate
- _____ Volleyball
- _____ Wrestling
- _____ Track

I/We realize that such activity involves the potential for injury which is inherent in all sports/activities. I/We acknowledge that even with the best coaching, use of the most advanced protective equipment, and strict observation of rules, injuries are still a possibility. On rare occasions, these injuries can be so severe as to result in total disability, brain damage, paralysis, quadriplegia, or even death.

I/We agree to accept these risks as a condition of participation

_____   _____
Parent/Guardian Signature   **Date**

INSURANCE (Please fill out the applicable section.)

1. I/We currently have insurance that will cover this student:

_____   _____
Name of Insurance Company   **Policy Number**

_____   _____
Parent/Guardian Signature   **Date**

2. School Insurance Coverage
This school district annually identifies an insurance company that provides accident insurance for parents of students that choose to participate and do not have or want additional insurance.
My signature indicates that I have purchased accident insurance through the school.

_____   _____
Parent/Guardian Signature   **Date**

3. Insurance Waiver
My signature below indicates that I am aware of the risk of injury and/or death that may result from athlete participation. I fully understand that the District strongly recommends that all students be covered by insurance and that the District is not financially responsible for injuries that may result from participation.
By signing below, I hold harmless this school district, it's coaching personnel, Administration, and Board for my decision to not have insurance for my student listed above.

_____   _____
Parent/Guardian Signature   **Date**

ALLERGIES: _____
MEDICATIONS NOW TAKING: _____

Extracurricular activities also offer opportunities to make new friends and develop relationships with people your child might otherwise not have associated with. As she interacts with a broader spectrum of people and learns about different ethnicities, lifestyles, and customs, your teen will become more tolerant and accepting of others. Increasing tolerance is a key strategy for combating school violence. The more students learn about different people and cultures, the less likely they will be to act aggressively against others simply because they are "different."

Establishing Individuality and Community

Extracurricular activities are also an important way students establish their individuality, because the clubs and teams they belong to help express and cultivate what's unique and interesting about them. At the same time that extracurricular activities help students establish individuality, they also help students form important bonds with others who share similar interests. Your teen may even shift her primary social group after she begins an activity, spending most of her time, for example, with fellow gymnasts or chess fanatics.

Finding a group of peers who share her interest offers an important validation for your teen, who wants to be different but also wants to "fit in." Thus, extracurricular activities help eighth graders understand who they are as individuals while at the same time creating a sense of community and connection to others.

Increased Self-Esteem

Participation in extracurricular activities gives students many opportunities for personal achievements that can dramatically boost self-esteem. Remember, for example, how proud you were when your basketball team won the playoffs, or how performing in *Guys and Dolls* gave you the confidence to speak more in the classroom and express yourself more around others? As a club or team member, your teen can contribute ideas, learn new skills, and improve old ones. Your child can become a leader (team captain or club officer), act as a teacher (help someone else learn or improve skills), enjoy the thrill of victory or the appreciation of an audience, or simply enjoy great satisfaction from carrying out tasks for the club or team.

> **Extracurricular activities were a real lifesaver for all six of my kids when they were in eighth grade. Sports gave them an outlet for their frustrations and helped them build their confidence, especially if they weren't particularly strong in school.**
>
> **—A PARENT FROM NORTH WALES, PENNSYLVANIA**

Cooperation and Responsibility

As a member of a supervised and structured group, your teen will also learn how to better communicate and cooperate with others, for the group's goals can only be met if everyone works together. He will learn that, as part of a team, he has a responsibility to his teammates. He will understand, for example, that if he doesn't lay out the pages for the literary magazine by Sunday, the group will miss its print deadline. He will also learn that, as part of a school-related activity, he also represents his school and is therefore responsible for behaving appropriately.

Service-oriented clubs will also help your teen develop higher levels of civic responsibility and show him that he can have fun while performing important (perhaps even life-saving) services for others. Your teen can get in valuable time with his friends while cleaning up a local park or preparing food in a soup kitchen, and he can see the immediate results of a team effort as he surveys the tidy park or hands a tray of food to a hungry person.

Discipline and Creativity

If your teen participates in an extracurricular activity that involves competition, such as being a member of the soccer team, or one that involves creating an end product, such as a yearbook, she will learn discipline and focus by working diligently toward a specific goal. As an athlete, for example, your teen will learn that to succeed, he will have to focus on improving specific skills, and that the only way to improve skills is to practice, practice, practice. Many extracurricular activities will also foster development of your teen's creativity by offering opportunities for problem solving, self-exploration, and self-expression, especially in creative and performing arts clubs. In a drama club, for example, your teen will learn how to convey emotions and ideas through improvisation and the production of plays.

Time Management

Teachers and parents of eighth graders point out that time management is often one of the biggest problem areas for eighth graders. Fortunately, this is another area in which extracurricular activities can help. Being involved in activities outside the classroom forces students to pay careful attention to their schedules and to carefully plan their time. They will learn that they have to meet deadlines in order to make things happen for their organization, and they will learn that poor time management can have serious consequences, not just for themselves but for others.

> Many demands are placed on the average eighth grader today, and if organizational skills could be bottled and sold, someone would be very wealthy. However, the fact is that organizing time is a matter of self-discipline that comes with the desire to succeed and the passion to learn. Part and parcel of organizational skills is a matter of modeling by parents and teachers. From that point on, it's the eighth grader's choice. Like every other good lesson taught to children, you can only hope that they choose to imitate the successful people they interact with on a daily basis.
>
> —MARGUERITE HARTILL, A FORMER MIDDLE SCHOOL PRINCIPAL
> FROM LONG ISLAND, NEW YORK

Keeping Kids Out of Trouble

In addition to personal development, many extracurricular activities play another important role in your child's life: they offer supervised, structured activities after school, the time of the day when adolescents are most likely to experiment with drugs, alcohol, and sex. And because they're supervised by school faculty and staff, teens have the opportunity to develop close personal relationships with teachers and counselors who can provide additional encouragement and support.

Avoid Risky Behavior

A study conducted by the Department of Health and Human Services found that participation in extracurricular activities significantly decreased the chances of risky behaviors among teens. According to the study, students who *do not* participate in extracurricular activities are:

- ❐ 57% more likely to drop out of school by their senior year
- ❐ 49% more likely to use drugs
- ❐ 37% more likely to become teen parents
- ❐ 35% more likely to have smoked cigarettes

than teens who spend one to four hours per week in extracurricular activities.

SOURCE: *ADOLESCENT TIME USE, RISKY BEHAVIOR, AND OUTCOMES: AN ANALYSIS OF NATIONAL DATA*, DEPARTMENT OF HEALTH AND HUMAN SERVICES, SEPTEMBER 1995.

Mentors and Role Models

Because extracurricular activities are supervised by school faculty and staff, and because parents are often involved as volunteers, teens have the opportunity to develop close personal relationships with teachers, counselors, and other adults who can serve as mentors and positive role models. Mentors can offer invaluable guidance and support, especially for teens who are struggling with low self-esteem. For example, your teen may become good friends with the assistant principal, who is also the advisor to the Spanish Club, and the assistant principal's attention to your child and his blooming Spanish language skills can give him the confidence he needs to succeed not just at club events but in all areas of his life. The more your teen is respected by adults whom *he* respects, the more likely your teen is to develop a healthy self-respect.

Parents Benefit, Too

Finally, extracurricular activities don't just benefit the teens who participate—they benefit parents, too. Extracurricular activities offer numerous opportunities for you to get involved: opportunities to encourage and support your teen when things don't work out as planned, opportunities to praise and reward your teen for work well done. This kind of involvement, of course, demonstrates that you care, and this in turn will further enhance your child's self-esteem. Extracurricular activities also allow you to connect with your child— perhaps you share that interest, too—and to connect with other parents, with whom you can share information, ideas and concerns.

All of this adds up to a child who has a more developed sense of self and a healthier attitude toward himself, toward others, and toward school.

KINDS OF EXTRACURRICULAR ACTIVITIES

OF course, the specific experiences and benefits your child will receive depends upon the type of extracurricular activity (or activities) she chooses. And chances are she will have lots of choices. The extracurricular activities at your child's school will likely fall into one of two categories: athletics or clubs. Most middle schools offer at least a half dozen clubs in addition to several competitive sports for each gender.

Athletics

1. **Interscholastic Competitive Sports**. In interscholastic competitive sports, your child's team will compete with teams from other schools. Teams are usually large, and the pressure to succeed (to win) can sometimes be high, but so can the rewards. These teams are usually extremely well organized with strict rules and high expectations for participation and

sportsmanship. There's more responsibility, but there's also more room for glory.

Your child will be expected to attend practice three to five days a week after school during the season and occasionally to attend games, meets, or practice sessions on weekends. Participation on such a team will require a major time commitment for the length of the season and may require some monetary investment in uniforms or equipment.

The competitive sports offered will vary from school to school, of course. At the middle school level they often include:

➤ Baseball (boys)
➤ Basketball
➤ Field hockey (girls)
➤ Football (boys)
➤ Gymnastics
➤ Ice hockey (boys)
➤ Indoor and outdoor track
➤ Lacrosse
➤ Soccer
➤ Softball (girls)
➤ Swimming
➤ Tennis
➤ Volleyball
➤ Wrestling (boys)

Extracurricular activities absolutely unequivocally had a positive impact on my son. He was generally quiet, but was a good athlete. Participating in sports (soccer, basketball, and baseball) gave him an outlet to build his self-confidence, interact with other kids, and develop leadership skills. His personality changed when he got out on the field.

—A PARENT FROM WEST ORANGE, NEW JERSEY

2. **Intramural Sports**. Rather than competing with students from other schools, intramural athletes compete against their own classmates. Teams are usually small and many different sports

are offered throughout the year. Intramural sports offer competition but without the pressure of competitive interscholastic sports. They tend to be less structured and are much less of a time commitment. Your teen won't have to practice everyday after school for three months. In fact, for many intramural sports, there's no formal practice sessions at all. Intramural athletes usually don't have a coach, either, though they will have trained referees for their sporting events. Many of the same interscholastic competitive sports are offered as intramural sporting activities, though typically intramurals focus on sports that require little equipment and fewer resources (such as trainers and referees).

3. **Club**. Athletic clubs actually fit into both major extracurricular activity categories—they're clubs organized around a sporting activity. Athletic clubs are usually not competitive. Instead, they meet to practice a sport, such as cycling, skiing, or golf, for the fun of it or to prepare for and participate in tournaments or special events, such as a charity bike race.

Clubs

There are as many different kinds of clubs as there are people. School clubs, however, typically fall into one of the following categories:

1. **Academic**. These clubs are about a specific academic skill or subject, such as math, history, or environmental science. One middle school, for example, offers a Weather Club. Students create daily weather maps using data from their own weather station and then broadcast their forecast on the school's PA. Competitive debate clubs, for example, which help teens develop their public speaking, critical thinking, and argumentation skills, are particularly popular in middle and high schools. Your child may also be able to join a Homework Club—a kind of after-school study hall—or an honors club that rewards and encourages students of outstanding academic achievement.

2. **Creative and Performing Arts.** The most common kind of club in middle schools around the nation, these clubs offer students

a chance to explore and improve their skills in a variety of creative and performing arts. Your child's school may offer a drama club, chorus, band, orchestra, dance club, photography club, and other groups.

3. **Leadership**. Students can develop leadership skills by participating in student government and other leadership organizations. Student councils often participate in regional or state activities throughout the year and serve as a hands-on introduction to the political process. Other leadership groups may include peer counseling or conflict mediation teams, through which students learn to help others resolve conflicts.

4. **Service**. These clubs may arrange for community service, where students volunteer through local or national organizations and serve others by visiting the elderly, delivering food to the hungry, and so on, or offer opportunities for school service, where students can serve as mentors for younger students or help others through a tutoring program. Service organizations are particularly good for helping students develop a sense of responsibility to others and learning how gratifying it can be to do good.

5. **Publications**. Most middle schools produce at least one student-run publication, such as a yearbook (the most common), a newspaper (usually one issue per month or per marking period), or a literary magazine (usually one or two issues per school year). These clubs aren't just for writers; publications also need students to take photographs, design covers, arrange page layouts, raise funds, and promote the publication.

> In 1994, middle school students at Centennial Middle School in Boulder, Colorado, created *The Vocal Point*, the world's first electronic student newspaper. Centennial students collaborate with students from other schools in Colorado, Minnesota, Oklahoma, Texas, and Canada to cover important issues, such as cloning and technology in schools, from a stu-

dent perspective. Visit the award-winning site at http://bvsd.k12.co.us/cent/Newspaper/index.html.

6. **Technology**. If your child's school doesn't offer a course in computers or educational technology, there may be a club that provides similar instruction. Other technology clubs may focus on specific computer software or tools, such as the Internet, computer games, or graphic design. Still other clubs may focus on multi-media or audio-visual programs and equipment.

7. **Cultural**. Many middle schools offer clubs devoted to exploring and celebrating particular cultures. If there is a large ethnic group in your teen's school, that group may be represented by a club through which students can explore their heritage and maintain cultural traditions. Other schools may offer a Diversity Club in which students learn about and celebrate multiple cultures.

8. **Business/Entrepreneurial**. These clubs offer students a chance to learn about and practice basic economic and business principles. Activities may include running the school store, running a mock stock exchange, or developing a small business. For example, students in a Young Entrepreneur's Club may see a business opportunity in creating customized book covers for classmates. They might conduct market research, write a business plan, and market their product.

Of course, there are still other kinds of clubs that don't fit neatly into any of these categories, such as a Craft Club or Chess Club. And many schools also offer extracurricular activities in the form of field trips and other outings. In addition, your child has many opportunities for extracurricular involvement through religious organizations, youth groups (such as the Boy Scouts), and other institutions that offer instruction in various areas, such as dance, music, karate, and so on. These activities offer the same benefits as extracurricular activities at school—increased self-esteem, improved social skills, better time management, and so on. School-sponsored extracurricular activities, however, offer two advantages: they require little or no cost for participation, and participation in school activities strengthens the bond both you and your child have with the school community.

Special Interest Clubs

Does your teen wish there were a club that dealt with one of her special interests? Why not help her start one? In many schools, a small group of students may petition to create a new club. They will need to explain the goals of the organization and the typical activities that will take place when the group meets. They will also need the support of at least one faculty member who will serve as advisor to the group and who can help them get the club off the ground.

HELPING YOUR CHILD CHOOSE

WITH so many options for extracurricular activities, how can you help your child decide which clubs to join? First, it's important to remember that extracurricular participation should be *your child's choice*, not yours. While you and your teen may share some interests, your child is his own person and needs to feel that this important decision is *his*. He needs the freedom to explore the things that interest him, and forcing your child to participate when he doesn't want to can create a great deal of unnecessary and unwanted resentment.

But that doesn't mean you should let your child sign up for any random activity. Your teen will benefit most if he chooses activities that match his talents, interests, and schedule. As you talk with your teen about extracurricular participation, keep the following questions in mind:

Choosing the Right Activity

1. What are your teen's strengths and weaknesses? Are there any interests your child would like to develop or explore?
2. Is there an interest or talent your child has that isn't covered (or covered in sufficient depth) in school?

3. What will the activity entail in terms of time and effort? Will he be able to meet his commitment to the group and manage the group's schedule?

4. What other responsibilities does your child have? Will he be able to keep up with those other responsibilities if he joins this group?

5. Will you be able to be at least minimally involved? If your work schedule will prevent you from attending most games, for example, will you be able to attend a practice here and there, or help organize the end-of-the-season awards banquet?

6. What behaviors or traits will be reinforced through this activity? For example, will the activity help your teen develop his teamwork, creativity, coordination, civic responsibility, or interpersonal or technical skills?

Avoid Over-Commitment

The biggest danger of extracurricular activities for many teens is over-commitment. "My daughter participates in several activities, and some nights she's up until one or two o'clock in the morning trying to get her work done," one parent reports. "She's benefiting tremendously from her participation, but she's also getting precious little sleep. I'm worried about her health." Indeed, evidence suggests that many adolescents are seriously over-committed and that sleep deprivation among adolescents is becoming a major concern for many families. With the intense physical growth and important physical changes happening to your teen's body—along with the amount of physical energy the typical teen expends, especially if he participates in sports—sufficient rest needs to be a top priority.

Over-commitment can also lead to academic woes. While most athletes and club members earn, on average, higher marks than students who don't participate, the over-committed student may see grades go down instead of up because she's overloaded. It's important for you and your teen to know how much she can handle and to know when to give up an activity if her schedule becomes too crowded. As important as extracurricular activities are, and as much as they help teens develop physically, socially, and academically, their regular academic curriculum must come first.

SUMMARY

THOUGH extracurricular activities are officially "outside" of the middle school curriculum, they're an essential part of the eighth grade experience. Extracurricular clubs and athletic teams offer the following benefits to teens:

- ➤ They increase knowledge and tolerance.
- ➤ They help teens establish their identity.
- ➤ They help teens feel like they're part of a community.
- ➤ They increase self-esteem.
- ➤ They promote cooperation and responsibility.
- ➤ They help develop discipline and creativity.
- ➤ They help teens learn how to manage their time.
- ➤ They help keep teens out of trouble.
- ➤ They create important opportunities for parental involvement.

Extracurricular activities include sports and clubs of all kinds, and while it's important to let your teen choose which teams or clubs to join, you can guide her by helping her consider her strengths and weaknesses, identify her interests, and determine whether or not she can manage the time commitment and other responsibilities of participation.

chapter 4

How to Support Learning at Home

EACH YEAR as your child has grown, he has become more and more independent, capable of doing so much more on his own. He seems to need you less and less as you see each other less often. Sometimes you may even begin to feel a little—well—unnecessary and unwanted. But during these critical adolescent years, your role as a parent is just as important as ever. It's not time to be less involved; it's just time to be involved in a slightly different way. As your teen moves closer and closer to adulthood, he will need you to step back from your role as caretaker and step further into your role as "coach," teaching strategies and providing plenty of guidance and support while letting your teen make more and more decisions on his own. And though during these years your adolescent may act like he doesn't care much about what you say or do, the fact is that your actions and attitude have a profound influence on your teen. This is especially true of your attitude toward education.

Obviously, you care deeply about your child's education, or you wouldn't be reading this book. And that's good news, because the biggest factor in a child's success at school is not the quality of the school or its instructors, the economic or social status of the family, or the education level of her parents. The key to student success is parental involvement and attitude. And because eighth grade is such an important year academically and socially, what you do—or don't do—this year will have a major impact on your child's success in school.

To support your eighth grader's academic efforts, you will need to create an environment in which education is respected and in which schoolwork is always a priority. Your home should also be a place where active learning is always taking place. This chapter will explain how you can create that kind of learning environment, how you can help your teen with homework, and what you can do at home to reinforce the skills your teen is learning in school.

> When my son was little I always read to him, but as he got older, he outgrew it. At the time I thought that was the only way to support his learning at home. Soon after, I learned from his teachers how important my support at home means to his education. Just by talking with him about what he is learning, by helping him with his homework, and by providing new and challenging ideas and experiences, I am doing a lot to increase his knowledge and making him a better student.
>
> —A PARENT FROM BOULDER, COLORADO

HOMEWORK

FOR years now, your child has been bringing home schoolwork, and by the eighth grade she is probably being assigned about two hours worth of homework each evening. If you're like most parents, you probably take the fact of homework for granted, and it may have been a while since you stopped to consider why teachers assign homework (especially so much of it) in the first place. After all, your teen is already in school for at least seven hours a day—why cut into family time and other activities with more schoolwork? The answer is simple: Homework is just plain good for your child.

The Benefits of Homework

The most obvious benefit of homework is its impact on academic success. Homework assignments

> ➤ review and reinforce material covered in class
> ➤ give students the opportunity to apply or practice the skills they learned in class
> ➤ allow students to explore more fully topics that were discussed in the classroom

As a result, students who regularly complete homework have a greater understanding of the material, and this results in higher grades and better test scores. In fact, research by the Department of Education shows a clear and strong correlation from the seventh grade on, between homework and scores on standardized tests.

Homework also helps build several skills critical for academic success. Assignments teach students how to

> ➤ use important resources, such as encyclopedias, atlases, the Internet, and dictionaries
> ➤ work independently to accomplish specific tasks
> ➤ take responsibility for their learning
> ➤ manage time effectively

In addition, homework has these important added benefits:

> ➤ It creates contact between parents and children and between parents and teachers.
> ➤ It increases self-esteem by giving students a daily sense of accomplishment of meaningful tasks and pride in understanding material.

How Much Homework Is Too Much?

Many parents wonder whether their teen is getting too much homework—or not enough. By the eighth grade, experts agree that students should be spending an average of two hours per school day doing homework. (If you think that sounds like a lot, consider this: students in China and Japan often receive four to five times as much homework!)

Despite these benefits, homework may not always be interesting and fun, and adolescents will understandably prefer to spend their time hanging out with friends or listening to music rather than doing homework. Generally, eighth grade homework assignments will be more rigorous and less playful than in the past, and eighth graders may be frustrated by assignments that challenge them to think more abstractly and master increasingly difficult skills. When students, especially adolescents, have repeated difficulty understanding homework, they may react by giving up on school, which of course only exacerbates the problem. According to the National Education Association, a recent survey of high school dropouts showed that an inability to keep up with homework was a critical factor in their decision to drop out of school. Your support on this front is therefore crucial.

Set Clear Rules and Expectations

One of the most important things to do is to establish clear rules regarding homework. Make sure your child knows that homework is a priority and knows exactly what you expect in terms of when, where, and how his homework will get done each day. For example, you may expect homework to be done immediately after school, at home or in the library, with no television, computer, or video games until the work is completed. The details of your homework policy will depend upon your teen's and your schedule. Be as consistent as possible, but do remember that you will need to allow for exceptions, such as when a special school activity is scheduled during your child's regular homework time.

If there doesn't seem to be enough time in your teen's day to complete homework assignments, you and your teen will need to take a good look at his schedule. Does he seem to have too many outside activities filling up his day? If so, he may need to drop one of those activities; homework must come first. If not, consider whether your teen needs to improve his time management skills or whether you need to talk to your teen's teachers about possible homework overload.

Your teen should know, too, what you expect in terms of academic performance. Of course, we'd all like our children to earn top grades, but not every student can be strong in every subject. It's important to have high but realistic expectations of your child and convey those expectations clearly. For example, if you consistently tell your child that she only needs to maintain a C average, she might only work as hard as it takes to get that C and no harder—not because she isn't capable of getting an A or B, but because she's simply living up to your expectations. Your child may begin to believe that she *can't* do any better than a C because that's all that you expect from her.

At the same time, however, be sure to be realistic. Although our culture places a high premium on grades, remember that what's important is not the specific grade your child earns but that he is working to the best of his ability. If you know your child is capable of A work in most of his classes, then it's fair to expect that he earn mostly A's on his report card. But if your child has an intrapersonal intelligence, for example (see "Learning Styles and Multiple Intelligences" on page 75), he may encounter some difficulty with math or science. If you then demand an A in every class from your child, you may be setting him up for serious problems with school and with his self-esteem.

Create a Study Area and Learning Environment

We are far more influenced by our surroundings than most of us realize. Soft lighting and neutral walls, for example, tend to help us feel calm and relaxed while lots of clutter and noise in a room often make it difficult for us to concentrate. To be productive, we usually need to be in relatively comfortable, quiet surroundings, and the more we associate a particular place with work, the more easily we slip into a productive mindset when we're in that area. A well-designed place set up specifically for schoolwork and a studious atmosphere can help get your teen into the right state of mind for effective learning.

Study Area

To be comfortable and productive during homework time, your teen should have a workspace that includes the following:

A desk or table and a comfortable chair. Make sure the desk or table is big enough for your teen to spread out her books and papers. The desk or table should also have drawers, shelves, boxes, or other compartments in which she can keep her supplies.

Sufficient lighting. There's no need for the harsh light of fluorescent bulbs, but your teen's workspace should be well lit to prevent eye strain and help improve concentration.

Tools and supplies. Your teen's work space should be well stocked with homework tools and supplies, including:

➤ a good dictionary, such as Merriam-Webster's Collegiate Dictionary, 10th Edition

➤ a thesaurus

➤ other reference materials, such as a world atlas, almanac, and an encyclopedia set, if possible

➤ paper (loose-leaf, sketch/drawing, as well as paper for the printer, if you have a computer)

➤ pencils and pencil sharpener, pens, highlighters, erasers, and white-out

➤ stapler and staples, paper clips, ruler, rubber bands

➤ folders, notebooks, and report covers

➤ glue, tape, scissors

➤ calculator

➤ calendar

Does My Teen Need a Computer?

Having a computer in your household may make it easier for your teen to complete some assignments, but she doesn't *need* one. Because no school can guarantee that each student has computer access outside of school, no teacher should assign homework that *requires* computer use unless students are also provided with class time in the computer lab to complete the assignment.

When it comes to homework, computers are particularly valuable tools for research, word processing, and document design. If you don't have a computer but your teen wants to use one after school for homework, check out the computer center at your local library.

Allow your teen some freedom to make his study area a very personal space. If his workspace is in his room, he can decorate accordingly. If his workspace is, for example, in your office or den, then help him personalize it by providing a bulletin board or desk pad on which he can tape or post personal items. The more personal it is, the more comfortable he will feel whenever he sits down to do work—which means he will be better able to concentrate.

Learning Environment

Once a workspace has been established, it's time to focus on atmosphere. The entire family will need to cooperate to create the right kind of environment for learning. That means there should be specific rules for behavior when someone is doing homework. Many parents find the following rules effective:

➤ **No television.** A teen who plops down in front of the television with her homework is not giving her work her full attention and not demonstrating that homework is a priority. If someone else is watching TV and the TV is within sight or within hearing, it is likely to be a major distraction.

➤ **No phone calls unless they are homework related.** Even a quick phone call from a friend can break your teen's concentration. Of course, some calls may be about homework, and it may be very helpful for your teen to talk an assignment through with a classmate. But beware: adolescents are notorious for long phone conversations, so even homework related calls should be kept short until the homework is finished.

➤ **No surfing the web except for research assignments and no computer games.** Computers can be a great help with homework, but they can also be a major distraction. Make it clear that there is to be no Internet browsing until after homework is completed unless the assignment requires research or other online help.

➤ **No interruptions unless they're urgent.** Ask siblings to leave your teen alone while he is working and avoid the temptation to interrupt him yourself. Most things you need to tell or ask your teen can wait until he's finished. Of course, if he asks for your help, you're not interrupting; you're providing needed support.

➤ **Quiet activities only while siblings are doing homework.** Ask siblings to read or play quietly so that loud toys and activities don't distract your teen.

What about music?

Whether or not your child should listen to music while doing homework depends upon your child's learning style and personality. Some people work better with quiet background music, and in fact studies have shown that playing classical music in the background (particularly music of baroque composers such as Bach, Vivaldi, and Handel) can actually *improve* the mind's ability to learn. But loud music of any kind is likely to be too distracting.

Remember that hunger can also be a major distraction. A healthy snack before homework will often help your child be more productive.

Brain Food

Good nutrition is essential for effective learning, especially at this time of dramatic physical change. Be sure your child starts each school day with a healthy breakfast, even if she's in a great rush. She won't learn well if she's distracted by hunger, and she'll experience a blood sugar "crash" by second period if she eats a breakfast loaded with processed sugars, such as donuts and juice. (Read labels carefully. Most juice drinks actually contain less than 25% juice—the rest is water and added sugars!)

Healthy breakfast choices include the following foods:

- ❐ fruit
- ❐ yogurt
- ❐ granola
- ❐ low-sugar cereals (such as Cheerios or Corn Flakes) with low-fat milk and cut-up fruit (for added sweetness)
- ❐ whole wheat or multi-grain toast or muffin with peanut butter
- ❐ eggs
- ❐ low-fat milk or 100% juice

Don't forget a multivitamin to fully meet your teen's nutritional needs.

Similarly, though school lunches are designed to be nutritious, your growing teen will probably need more fuel by mid-afternoon. Provide a healthy after-school snack, especially if your child usually does his homework right after school. Healthy snacks include:

- ❐ carrot and celery sticks
- ❐ fruit, especially bananas
- ❐ apple slices with peanut butter
- ❐ raisins
- ❐ granola bars
- ❐ nuts
- ❐ zucchini, carrot, or banana bread
- ❐ fruit smoothies

❒ string cheese or cheese slices

❒ mini-pizzas (spread pasta sauce on a halved English muffin, sprinkle generously with shredded mozzarella cheese, and pop in the oven)

Avoid foods high in processed sugars and caffeine, though it's best not to forbid them altogether (that's likely to make your child want them all the more). Besides, if your teen eats a well-balanced diet on a regular basis, it's okay to offer an occasional high-sugar or high-calorie treat.

Remember that especially at this age, your actions will speak louder than your words. A "Do as I say, not as I do" approach will likely backfire with your teen. If you want your child to eat well, *you* need to eat well, too.

Make Homework a Family Activity

One of the best ways to ensure that your teen has the right atmosphere for homework is to make homework a family activity. If you and your children all sit down to do some work for an hour or so after school or after dinner, then everyone will be busy with his or her own tasks, creating a quiet and cooperative learning environment. Plus, if you're doing "homework," too, you will be setting a good example for your teen and demonstrating that many of the skills he's learning in school are skills he will use throughout his lifetime.

What kind of homework can you do? If you've brought work home from the office, do that. You can also pay bills, write letters, research products you're interested in purchasing for the home, find out how to repair a household item, prepare a budget, research investments, put together shopping lists, or read for work or pleasure.

Be Involved

The older your child gets, the more complex the material he will be learning in school—and the more intimidated you may feel about getting involved. "How can I help?" asks one eighth grade parent. "It's been 20 years since I studied algebra." Another parent worries about the changing curriculum: "I took physics in high school, but my child is studying a very different kind of physics today. I'm afraid I'll teach her the wrong thing." And of course many parents are afraid of "looking stupid" in front of their children if they don't know the correct answers.

The only "stupid" thing, though, is to not get involved. It's ok if you don't know all the answers or can't solve all of the equations. What matters is that you are there to help your child learn *how to find* the right answers. For example, if your teen is stuck on a quadratic equations assignment but you don't remember a whit of algebra, don't despair. Instead, turn your ignorance into a great "teachable moment." Ask your teen to explain everything about quadratic equations that she does understand and ask her to show you how she solved similar problems. Then, together, you can use her knowledge and the information in the textbook to come up with the correct answer. With this approach, you may not have to do much more than listen. Often, when students start explaining a concept, they realize they understand it better than they think they do—and they can solve the problem on their own after all. Needless to say, this kind of experience is a great confidence booster: Your teen solved a difficult problem, and you cared enough to provide support.

Here are some specific ways you can be more involved with your teen's schoolwork:

> ➤ **Show your support.** Make sure your child knows you're available for help. If you're not home when your child is doing homework, make it clear that you will set aside time to review his work when you get home.
> ➤ **Know what your child's assignments are** and what the homework policy is for each class. What kinds of assignments will teachers give? How often will they give homework? How much time is your teen expected to spend on assignments? What type of parental involvement is expected?
> ➤ **Communicate regularly with your child's teachers.** Stay in touch even if there doesn't seem to be any problem. If you

communicate regularly, you're more likely to prevent problems *before* they occur. If you have any concerns about the assignments or your child's ability to complete them, communicate those concerns to your teen's teachers immediately. Let teachers know if your child is finding the work too difficult or too easy. Teens need to be challenged; a teen who is bored with schoolwork is more likely to develop disciplinary and attitude problems in school than one who is being pushed to reach his or her potential.

➤ **Know your teen's learning style and primary intelligence** (see the box on page 77). This can help you set up a more effective learning environment and establish guidelines that are appropriate for your teen. For example, if your teen is a kinesthetic learner, don't punish her for not being able to sit still for two hours of straight study time. Instead, encourage her to get up and stretch every 20 minutes to refocus her energy. Knowing your child's learning style will also help you more effectively explain concepts to your teen and better understand why she may have difficulty with certain subjects.

➤ **Help your teen manage her time.** Set up a calendar that lists your child's assignments and exams. When she has a major project, help her break down the project into manageable tasks and schedule each step. This will teach her effective time management skills and help prevent procrastination and last-minute cramming for exams.

➤ **Check over your child's work** to be sure it's complete, and whenever possible, help him check his work for errors. Don't correct mistakes for him; instead, point them out and guide him as necessary so that he can figure out how to correct mistakes himself.

Sufficient Shut-Eye

If your teen is having trouble with schoolwork or seems unable to concentrate on assignments, it could be a sign that he's not getting enough rest. According to a recent study reported on Cosmiverse.com, "a large percentage of children near puberty are exhibiting symptoms of sleep deprivation on a more consistent basis." Experts recommend that adolescents get 9–10 hours of sleep each night, but surveys of middle and high school students show that most teens only get between 6–8 hours of sleep during the school week. This lack of sleep can have serious consequences for your child, including poor concentration, impaired memory, inhibited creativity, and extra emotional sensitivity.

Adolescent lack of sleep may be due to an over-booked schedule, but even teens with light schedules are likely to have some trouble getting enough sleep. And puberty is partly to blame. Changes in the body during puberty may disrupt your adolescent's circadian rhythms (sleeping patterns), so even if your child goes to bed at 10:00, he may lie awake staring at the ceiling for several hours. Unfortunately, on school days, he can't sleep in, and you'll be faced with an extra-groggy teen in the morning.

Because so many teens don't get enough rest during the week, it's common for them to try to catch up on the weekends. Your weekend schedule may be full and you may feel that a teen who doesn't get up until noon is just being lazy, but that extra few hours on Saturday and Sunday may be extremely important for your child if she needs to make up for a sleep deficit accumulated during the week. Whenever possible, let your child catch up on his rest.

Source: "Sleep Deprivation among Adolescents," *Science News*, (www.cosmiverse.com/ science052301.html), May 23, 2000.

Have a Positive Attitude about Education and Homework

Even when the going gets tough and you and your child are struggling with homework issues, keep your positive attitude about schoolwork. Make it clear that you support the efforts of your child's school—and of your child. Be especially careful to avoid questioning a teacher's authority or criticizing a teacher in front of your teen. If you express disdain for school, your child will, too. But if you show respect for teachers and the educational process, your child will model that behavior.

Criticism and Praise

We all know from our own experience how much sincere praise can boost our self-esteem—and how quickly criticism can topple it. But that doesn't mean you shouldn't criticize your teen. Children need to know when their work doesn't measure up or when they're not performing to the best of their ability.

The key is to offer **constructive criticism** that points out the specific problem *without placing blame on your teen*. Here's an example:

Destructive criticism:	You sure did a lousy job on this essay.
Constructive criticism:	Your report was difficult for me to follow. You seem to be trying to prove several different points and I'm not sure which one is your main idea.
Destructive criticism:	You really bombed this practice exam.
Constructive criticism:	From the errors on your practice exam, it looks like you're having trouble figuring out area and volume.

Notice how the constructive comments *describe the problem*, which enables the recipient to focus on the problem and how to correct it rather than on what may be wrong with *him*.

Of course, be sure to praise your child for work well done whenever possible. Remember that praise, like criticism, should be specific. "Good work" is nice, but "You did a great job explaining your hypothesis and organizing your data" is far, far better. When you're specific, you let your teen know the precise behaviors or attitudes that merit praise. When she knows exactly what she's done right or doing well, she will be more likely to repeat those positive behaviors.

HOMEWORK DO'S AND DON'T'S

Do	Don't
Be available to help.	Do your teen's homework. It may be difficult to watch your child struggle with an assignment, but you should never do your child's work for him. This will not only keep him from understanding and applying what he's learned in school, it will also undermine his self-esteem by making him feel that he's not capable of doing it himself.
Help your child make sure he understands the assignment. Ask questions such as: ❏ "Do you understand what you're supposed to do for this assignment?" ❏ "Do you need help understanding the work?" ❏ "What needs to be done to complete this assignment?" (This helps your child break down the assignment into specific manageable tasks.) ❏ "Do you have everything you need to do the work?" ❏ "Have you seen any assignments or problems like this one before?"	Use homework as a punishment or allow your child to skip homework as a reward.

I Saw That!

We're often quick to tell our children when they do something wrong while we tend to take their good behavior for granted. Make an effort to "catch" your teen doing something right each day and praise that behavior. For example, even if you expect your teen to set the table each night for dinner, *thank* him for it when he follows through: "I appreciate your setting the table. It makes preparing dinner much easier for me." Just because it's a household chore doesn't mean it doesn't deserve appreciation. (Think about how good it feels for you when your family members thank you for making dinner, mowing the lawn, or folding the laundry.)

LEARNING STYLES AND MULTIPLE INTELLIGENCES

RESEARCH over the last several decades has made it very clear that people process information in different ways and that to be successful, classroom practices need to accommodate all types of learners. There are three main learning styles:

Visual learners learn best by seeing; they often think in pictures and mental images. They tend to prefer information presented in visual displays, such as illustrations and diagrams, maps, tables, charts, and videos.

Auditory learners learn best by hearing and listening; they like to talk things through and listen to others explain ideas. They are adept at picking up tone and other subtleties of speech and benefit greatly from reading out loud. In fact, written texts will often not make much sense to auditory learners until they *hear* it.

Kinesthetic learners learn best through hands-on interaction. They prefer to *do* rather than look or listen. They like activity and exploration, and as a result they often find it hard to sit still for long stretches of time.

Different classroom methods tend to benefit different kinds of learners:

Learning Mode	Classroom Method
Visual learning mode:	textbooks, maps, illustrations, tables/charts
Auditory learning mode:	lectures and discussions
Kinesthetic learning mode:	experiments, building, or craft projects

We are all able to process information to some degree through each learning style, but most of us have a strong preference for one type of learning. Which type of learner is your teen? If you know *how* your teen learns best, you can use that knowledge to better explain ideas to your child. For example, if your kinesthetic learner is having difficulty memorizing a map of Native American territories because she is not a visual learner, you might suggest that she draw her own map and cut it up into puzzle pieces. The act of drawing and putting together the pieces will help her process the information she needs to know.

Knowing your teen's learning style can also help in other ways. If your teen seems to be having trouble with a particular subject, ask him to describe that teacher's methods. What typically happens in the classroom? It could be that your kinesthetic learner is struggling in a class where most of the material is covered in lectures and discussions. If there seems to be a mismatch between your child's learning style and a particular teacher's approach, make an appointment with that teacher. Teachers *want* students to succeed, and if they're aware of a problem reaching a particular student, they'll do their best to accommodate special learning needs.

Another way to classify how your teen learns is through the theory of **multiple intelligences** developed by Harvard educator Howard Gardner. Dr. Gardner believes that there are many different ways to define "intelligence" and that people can be "intelligent" in many different ways. There's the classic distinction, for example, between someone who is "book smart" and someone who is "street smart." Dr. Gardner proposes seven specific kinds of intelligence:

Intelligence	Brief Description
Visual-Spatial	Thinks in pictures and mental images. Good at puzzles, reading, writing, understanding visual displays of information, visual arts, design.
Verbal-Linguistic	Thinks in words rather than pictures. Good at listening, speaking, writing, explaining, storytelling, teaching, remembering information.
Logical-Mathematical	Thinks conceptually in logical and numerical patterns. Good at problem solving, classifying and categorizing information, working with abstractions, conducting controlled experiments, working with geometrical shapes.
Bodily-Kinesthetic	Expresses self through bodily movement and processes information by interacting with space. Good at dancing, sports, coordination, hands-on projects, using body language, acting, building, crafts.
Musical-Rhythmic	Thinks in sounds, rhythms, and patterns. Good at singing, playing musical instruments, writing music, recognizing tonal patterns, understanding the structure and rhythm of music, remembering melodies.
Interpersonal	Thinks about things from other people's points of view and uses empathetic ability to understand situations. Good at: seeing things from multiple perspectives, communicating, coordinating groups, cooperating with others, counseling, determining people's feelings and motivations, resolving conflicts.
Intrapersonal	Thinks about own feelings, dreams, and character; uses self-reflection to understand inner state of being. Good at: recognizing own strengths and weaknesses; analyzing feelings, desires, and dreams; reasoning with self; understanding relationships with others; evaluating thinking patterns and behaviors.

SOURCE: "FRAMES OF MIND" BY HOWARD GARDNER. COPYRIGHT © 1983 BY HOWARD GARDNER.

Most of us have one primary intelligence or dominant mode of thinking, but we all use multiple intelligences to process information and understand our world. Some of these modes of understanding will come naturally to your child; other modes may be very difficult for your teen. Consider your teen's favorite classes, her hobbies, her strengths and weaknesses. What is her primary way of understanding the world? If your teen is always listening to music, loves music class, and sings all the time, chances are she has a strong musical/rhythmic intelligence.

Once you've identified your teen's primary intelligence, you can once again use this knowledge to better support your teen. If your teen has a strong musical/rhythmical intelligence, for example, you can help him memorize information by creating a song that incorporates the material. Similarly, if your teen has a strong interpersonal intelligence, you can help her better understand historical events by asking her to imagine them from different people's points of view.

Turn Off the Tube!

If your teen isn't doing well in school, the culprit could be that "plug-in drug," the television. Numerous studies have established clear links between excessive television viewing and poor academic performance, as well as obesity, inhibited creativity, and poor physical fitness. Most estimates pin average adolescent TV time between two to four hours *per day*, with at-risk teens watching up to six hours daily.

One of the main problems with TV, of course, is that it is a passive activity. With a few good exceptions (many of which your child has long outgrown, such as *Sesame Street*), television requires very little thought or action from the viewer. Except for quality educational programming, television doesn't build any academic, physical, or social skills—and the more time spent in front of the tube, the more quickly those skills deteriorate.

What are the alternatives? It may be difficult, but you need to set major restrictions on TV time. Your children *will* thank you later—and maybe even sooner. Instead of watching TV, they'll engage in other, more constructive activities—like reading, sports, or other extracurricular activities.

While some parents choose to do away with television altogether, most find a happy medium by limiting TV to one hour a day except on special occasions (such as the World Series). You may also schedule exceptions for educational programming, such as a production on Masterpiece Theater. And you can certainly recommend that your teen watch shows about topics being covered in class.

To combat the passive nature of TV, whenever possible, sit down with your teen and watch a show with her. TV does offer good opportunities for discussion that *can* help your teen's social and emotional development. If you watch a sitcom, for example, ask your teen what he thinks about the behavior of the characters or what he might do in a similar situation.

SKILL-BUILDING AT HOME

OF course, learning doesn't just occur in school or during homework sessions. It happens all around, all the time—especially at home. You want your home to feel like *home*, not school, and you don't want your teen to feel like she's always studying, but you also want to reinforce and supplement what your child is learning in school. Fortunately, there are many things you can do to engage and educate your teen, often while getting in some quality family time. The remainder of this chapter will suggest specific activities for several subject areas that will help reinforce skills your teen is learning in school.

General Skills—Across the Curriculum

➤ To help your child with any subject, ask her to explain what she's learning to you. You can't teach someone material that you don't understand, so if your child can explain something clearly to you, that demonstrates that she understands it well. Explaining what she knows will reinforce and deepen her understanding. If she has difficulty explaining a concept, then she'll realize what she needs to review to better understand the material. Asking your child to explain will also strengthen her oral communication skills, which are increasingly important in the eighth grade. You can encourage her to use her learning style, too. For example, if she's a visual learner, ask her to draw or map out the concept she's explaining.

➤ To help your child become a more critical thinker, use everyday situations to develop her argumentation skills. When she states an opinion, ask her to support it. For example, if your teen tells you that the movie she just saw was "really great," ask her to support that opinion with specific details. What was great about it? The story line? (What was it?) The characters? (What were they like?) The acting? (Were the characters believable?) Likewise, you can discuss more challenging topics to help your teen develop character and determine how she feels about moral issues, such as racism or war.

English

➤ Wherever you go, be it the museum or zoo, grocery store or gas station, encourage your teen to read signs, brochures, and pamphlets.

➤ Have your teen help you conduct research in the library or on the Internet. For example, if you are planning to make a major purchase, such as a new printer, your teen can help you find product descriptions and reviews as well as compare price quotes.

➤ Create a reading-rich environment. Have lots of books, magazines, and other reading materials around the house. Subscribe to a magazine about an area of your child's interest to encourage your child to read. (See Chapter 8 for suggestions.)

➤ Go to the library or bookstore together often. Find out if the library sponsors reading groups. The South Orange Library in New Jersey, for example, offers a wonderful "Club X"—a cross-generational reading group where adults and adolescents get together to discuss selected readings.

➤ Ask your child to narrate events, describing in detail what happened and how he felt. Ask questions to get him to be more descriptive. For example, if your child mentions a new friend, ask, "What does he look like?" This will also help your teen become more observant.

➤ Play word games, such as Scrabble or Boggle, or do crossword puzzles together. (This is a *great* way to get in some quality family time.)

➤ Give your child meaningful writing tasks, such as letters to family or friends, grocery lists, lists of guests to invite for a party. Lists of any kind can help build your child's organizational skills. When she prepares a list, ask her to group items by category.

➤ Encourage your teen to keep a journal or diary to record and explore her personal feelings and experiences. Be sure to respect her privacy! Remember how important it was to you if you kept a journal as a teen. She won't write as much, or won't write honestly, if she's worried that you'll peek.

➤ To help your child learn how to write effective and realistic dialogue, tape record a conversation. Then have your teen transcribe that conversation.

➤ Write a letter to the editor of your local paper with your teen about an issue that concerns both of you.

➤ Have your child write her own greeting cards instead of buying them.

➤ Start a family quote book or memory book in which you all record memorable sayings or experiences.

Math

➤ Help your teen see the importance of math in all areas of life. Point out how math is used in shopping, sports, travel, building, and other daily activities.

➤ Have your teen create a budget for her allowance or, if she works, her income. Ask for her help in budgeting holiday shopping or other major expenses.

➤ Determine measurements for household projects together, such as laying down a new carpet or planting a garden.

➤ Shopping and cooking offer numerous opportunities for practicing math. Estimate the total cost of items, calculate the difference in cost between comparable items, calculate calories in a certain number of servings, or determine measurements for a modified number of servings.

➤ Discuss statistical data in newspapers and reports. For example, find a survey about a subject of interest to your child, such as video games. Discuss how the data was gathered and represented statistically. What do the numbers mean? How are the numbers being used? What effect might they have?

➤ Play games that require math skills (even if those skills are very basic), such as Monopoly or Yahtzee.

Science

➤ Use the natural phenomena you experience and current events as opportunities to discuss science. For example, discuss the recent discovery of a new cancer drug or how to fix the broken pendulum on the clock.

➤ Help your child practice the scientific method by applying it to all kinds of situations. For example, determine a specific phenomenon, such as the fact that the shrubs in the front of the house do much better than those in the back, though they both get about the same amount of sun. Then determine a hypothesis and how you might go about testing that hypothesis.

➤ Watch Discovery, *Nova,* or other science-related channels or programs together.

➤ Visit science museums in your area.

➤ Discuss the ethical issues surrounding scientific discoveries (current and potential). For example, would your child support the cloning of humans? Why or why not?

➤ Explore genetics with your teen by analyzing family traits.

➤ Create a genetic map of inherited characteristics.

➤ Create a model of an atom or molecule with toothpicks and radishes or balls of clay.

➤ Visit local geological sites, such as a cavern, cliff, or quarry.

Social Studies

➤ Follow and discuss issues in local (or global) politics.

➤ Explore your family's history before and after arrival in the United States.

➤ Use democratic principles in the household. For example, hold a vote to determine where to dine on a family night out. (Of course, the person footing the bill has the power of veto!)

➤ Research the history of your area. When and how was it settled? By whom? Were there Native Americans there first? What happened to them? Did any significant historical events take place in or near your town?

➤ Visit local historical sites, such as a battlefield, historical home, or historical museum.

➤ If you live near a Native American reservation, visit the reservation.

➤ Watch and discuss films about topics covered in class. For example, when your teen is studying industrialization, rent Charlie Chaplin's *Modern Times* (chances are she's never seen a silent film before—and this classic is both highly educational and very entertaining).

➤ Ask your teen to imagine that she is living in a certain time period, such as 1864 or 1930. What would her life be like as different people—a young white boy? a 30-year-old black woman?

Computers/Technology

➤ Chances are your teen is more computer savvy than you. Have him teach you a new program, such as how to use spreadsheets for a family budget. Or, if neither of you know much about computers, take a class together at your local library, or learn a program together at home.

➤ Use the computer to create greeting cards, letterhead, and report covers.

➤ Use the computer to conduct research for family projects, such as where to go for a family vacation.

Foreign Language

➤ Ask your teen to teach you as she learns so you can practice the language together.
➤ Rent foreign films (with subtitles) to hear the language and learn about the culture.
➤ Find copies of familiar fairy tales in the language your teen is studying. Because the storyline is similar, it should be relatively easy to follow (and fun!).

Music

➤ Expose your teen to music of all kinds. Play jazz, rock-and-roll, classical music, opera; listen to genres that she enjoys, too—hip-hop, rap, and top 40 hits.
➤ To reinforce reading skills, buy the sheet music for songs that your child enjoys. Have him read along as the song is played.
➤ Play and discuss the music that you loved when you were a teen.
➤ Attend musical performances. Again, expose your teen to a variety of genres.
➤ Rent a musical or music documentary.

Art

➤ Have your teen create his own greeting cards and wrapping paper (decorate newsprint or tissue paper, wrap presents with old maps, or use decorative rubber stamps to create custom gift wrap).
➤ Have your teen make gifts (crafts, ceramics, etc.) for family and friends.
➤ Go to museums together and discuss the works with your teen (you can now visit most major museums online).

➤ Ask your teen to draw or paint a picture of her feelings.

➤ Explore public art in your area, such as sculptures, murals, statues, and landscaped plazas.

➤ Notice small ways that art and design improves the quality of life and point them out to your child—a stained glass window, the art hanging on the wall in the doctor's office, the way the colors of a house complement each other.

Physical Education/Health

➤ Discuss healthy practices—and model them.

➤ Turn on music and dance!

➤ Have your teen help with physically demanding chores, such as yard work.

➤ Plan nutritious meals together.

➤ Take a hike together. Go for family walks. You can use the time to talk or for quiet reflection as well as exercise.

Character Development

➤ Volunteer together.

➤ Praise your child when she treats others with respect.

➤ Use teachable moments to discuss moral issues and values-based decisions. For example, if you and your teen witness someone in the act of littering, pick up the trash together, if possible, and discuss the importance of a clean environment.

SUMMARY

AS your teen embarks on his most challenging school year yet, he's going to need lots of support from you at home. To help your teen succeed in school:

➤ Have a positive attitude about education and make learning a priority in the home.

➤ Set specific rules about homework and provide a comfortable, personal space for your child to study.

➤ Be available to help your teen with difficult assignments and have the whole family cooperate to create an effective learning environment.

➤ Encourage your teen to sleep and eat well and offer constructive criticism as well as plentiful and specific praise for accomplishments and good behavior.

➤ Determine your teen's learning style and dominant intelligence(s) so you can help him better understand and remember important concepts.

➤ Limit television time and encourage other activities to reinforce the skills your teen is learning in school.

Remember that though your teen will push for more and more independence throughout the year, she still needs you to be involved, and she will still be profoundly influenced by your actions and attitude. You still have the power to make a great deal of difference to your teen.

chapter 5

Standardized Tests in 8th Grade

ONE OF the most hotly contested issues in education today is standardized testing. The debate between critics and proponents has raged for decades, but now the controversy has reached a level of intensity that has put standardized tests in the national spotlight. In May of 2001, for example, a group of parents in Scarsdale, New York, led a widely publicized boycott of the state-mandated eighth grade reading and math tests. And it wasn't just parents who rebelled against the exam. Demonstrating his support of the dissenting parents, the district superintendent ordered teachers to stop using class time to help students prepare for the exams. Some 60% of eighth graders sat out the exams, and in the following weeks parents in other towns across the nation organized similar boycotts.

But are standardized tests really that bad? And, even if they are, what can you do to make the experience more meaningful for your teen? Before we look at the objections to standardized tests and explain how you can help your teen prepare for them, let's first review exactly what standardized tests are, why they were created, and why schools have been using them for decades.

STANDARDIZED TESTS:
WHAT THEY ARE, HOW THEY WORK

ON a **standardized test**, all test takers take the same exam or take one of several versions that offer questions at the same level of difficulty and cover similar material. A standardized test follows the same format and procedures and is scored in precisely the same way to ensure a fair evaluation and to allow for comparative measures. Thus, student scores can be compared within a school and among classrooms, and if the same test is used state wide, results can be compared from school to school and district to district.

There are two main types of standardized tests: **aptitude tests** and **achievement tests**. Aptitude tests attempt to measure a student's learning aptitude or innate ability for academic success. The Scholastic Aptitude Test (SAT), which is required for most college applicants, is the most recognizable example. (This is not to be confused with the Stanford Achievement Test, 9th Edition [SAT 9] that many states have adopted for their state standardized test.) Achievement tests, on the other hand, attempt to measure what a child has already learned without regard to his or her learning potential.

The standardized tests your teen will face this year, and the standardized tests that school administrators and politicians use to measure student and school performance, are achievement tests. Unlike most tests your child takes in school, these tests are created not by his teachers, but by test development companies that study state standards and develop tests that cover a wide range of required academic material. These companies involve educators and specialists in the process to try to create a test that fairly measures the level of achievement of the test-taking population.

Because standardized tests are often administered on such a large scale with tens or even hundreds of thousands of students taking the same exam, tests need to be scored quickly and accurately. As a result, most questions on standardized tests have been of the multiple choice variety. Even before computers, multiple-choice answer sheets could be quickly scanned and test scores tallied.

Adding a New Dimension

In response to the criticism that most multiple-choice questions test retention of facts and not skills and processes, most eighth grade achievement tests now include more open-ended test questions, such as short essay responses. The New York State math exam, for example, includes a section where students first come up with an answer to a word problem and then explain, in writing, how they came up with that answer. This allows educators to assess the student's thought process and give at least partial credit to the student if she approached the problem correctly, even if she didn't come up with the correct answer. (A sample open-ended math question is provided at the end of this chapter.)

The obvious advantage of open-ended questions is that students can explain what they know (or how they know what they know), and this reflects achievement in a very different and important way. The problem with this approach, however, is the inevitable inconsistency in the evaluation process. Unlike multiple-choice questions, which can be scored with complete objectivity, the assessment of written responses is necessarily subjective, even if evaluators use a detailed scoring rubric (such as the writing rubric described in Chapter 2). Still, open-ended questions have added an interesting and important new dimension to standardized tests, one that acknowledges multiple intelligences, as discussed in Chapter 4, and stresses the importance of communication.

Glossary of Terms

Have you heard certain words tossed around when discussing standardized tests? This short list of terms will help you understand what it all means.

Rubric: A rubric is used to score writing samples. Typically, it is a grid that lists the levels of achievement, such as content, development, organization, and conventions as well as the varying degrees of quality within those categories. Grades can range from zero to six, six being the highest score.

Prompt: A prompt is a statement/question that requires a writer to think and respond. There is no right or wrong answer for a writing prompt. However, a good piece of writing will be well-developed, comprehensible, and abide by the conventions of the English language.

Holistic Scoring: This is a method by which professionals evaluate a piece of writing for its overall quality. Generally, the grade is based on content, development, organization, and conventions.

Curriculum: A curriculum is a guide that states expected learning outcomes, required materials (textbooks, documents, etc.), goals, objectives, concepts, and skills to be used for a course of study.

Benchmark: Used on state testing, benchmarks are standards by which others are measured.

Achievement Test: A test that attempts to measure what a child has already learned without regard to his or her learning potential. An example of this would be to ask a child what 10 divided by two equals.

Aptitude Test: A test that attempts to measure a student's learning aptitude or innate ability for academic success. An example of this would be to ask a child to determine the meaning of an unfamiliar word by using the context of the word.

Norm-Referenced Test (NRT): A test that is designed specifically to compare students to each other. NRTs are designed to "rank-order" test takers—that is, to compare students' scores. A commercial norm-referenced test does not compare all the students who take the test in a given year. Instead, test-makers select a sample from the target student population (say, ninth graders). The test is "normed" on this sample, which is supposed to fairly represent the entire target population (all ninth graders in the nation). Students' scores are then reported in relation to the scores of this "norming" group. (www.fairtest.org)

Criterion-Based Test: A test that is designed specifically to determine whether children have mastered a body of knowledge. Criterion-referenced tests (CRTs) are intended to measure how well a person has learned a specific body of knowledge and skills. On a standardized CRT (one taken by students in many schools), the passing or "cut-off" score is usually set by a committee of experts. (www.fairtest.org)

State versus Federal Control

Currently each state controls standardized testing in its schools, as each state department of education determines specific educational standards and assessment procedures. Most states administer tests only in certain grades, often the fourth and eighth grades, but that's likely to change under the Bush administration. On just his second day in office, President Bush released his "No Child Left Behind" proposal for education reform, "Achieving Equality through High Standards and Accountability" (available at www.ed.gov/inits/nclb/part3.html). Though states would still have the power to establish their own standards and development their own exams, Bush's plan would require states to administer math and reading exams *each year* from third grade through eighth grade. The House of Representatives and the Senate have both passed their own versions of Bush's plan, and in the coming months committees will turn these resolutions into law.

WHY SCHOOLS USE ACHIEVEMENT TESTS

FOR decades now, schools have been relying on standardized tests as a means of monitoring the progress of students and schools. In any grade level, students should master a certain set of skills and attain a certain body of knowledge before they proceed to the next grade level. Because the curriculum and standards of individual teachers and schools can vary greatly, standardized tests have been used to ensure that all schools in a state or district are providing students with the required skills and knowledge for specific grade levels. The newest trend in this area is requiring achievement tests for graduation. Largely a response to criticism that students are graduating without possessing the skills and knowledge needed to succeed in college or in the workplace, 29 states are currently developing or have already implemented exit exams which high school students must pass in order to receive a diploma.

> **Requiring annual state assessments in math and reading in grades three through eight will ensure that the goals are being met for every child, every year. Annual testing in every grade gives teachers, parents, and policymakers the information they need to ensure that children will reach academic success.**
>
> **—PRESIDENT GEORGE W. BUSH,**
> **"ACHIEVING EQUALITY THROUGH HIGH STANDARDS AND ACCOUNTABILITY"**
> **EDUCATION REFORM PROPOSAL, JANUARY 2001.**

Standardized tests are also used to measure individual student achievement. Specifically, schools use standardized test scores to:

➤ report on student progress
➤ diagnose student strengths and weaknesses
➤ select students for special programs (such as gifted programs)
➤ place students into the appropriate track (for example, remedial, standard, or honors English)
➤ to certify student achievement (grade promotion, graduation)

Many educators view the last goal as particularly important for eighth graders, who need to be adequately prepared for the high school year to come.

Standardized tests are not just an important tool for measuring student achievement; they're also a primary measure of school performance. Specifically, achievement test results are used to:

➤ evaluate school programs, such as a district-wide interdisciplinary program
➤ evaluate overall performance of individual schools
➤ evaluate the overall performance of teachers

Results of standardized tests can help educators identify and address problems in particular schools and districts. If the average reading scores in a particular school are significantly lower than the state norm, for example, educators can investigate the cause and institute corrective measures, such as hiring more teachers to reduce class size or revamping the curriculum.

Content and Timing

Currently most standardized tests in eighth grade focus on math and reading skills, though increasingly science, social studies, health, and even the arts, are also covered, and some states are developing achievement tests for other content areas, including art, music, and foreign languages. Questions for each content area typically cover the specific skill/knowledge categories mandated by state standards. The Florida Comprehensive Assessment Test (FCAT), for example, measures math achievement in Number Sense, Measurement, Geometry and Spatial Sense, Algebraic Thinking, and Data Analysis and Probability, according to Florida state content standards. The questions themselves don't indicate the particular skill or sub-content being tested, but the test preparers tag each question so that the results can be broken down to reflect achievement in very specific categories.

Standardized tests are given at different times of the school year, depending upon state requirements. Math may be tested on one day, English the next, science a few days later. Many states require schools to administer tests about halfway through the school year, after the holiday break, so that strengths and weaknesses can be addressed through the remainder of the school year, while others test in April and May, allowing the tests to serve as a grade promotion and placement tool.

Each school district will have its own specific reasons for administering the test. Some may administer tests simply because it is state law, because, like the Scarsdale educators, they don't particularly believe in standardized tests as a means of measuring achievement. In other school districts, your teen will be taking the test because administrators want to use it to evaluate a revised curriculum, to measure teacher effectiveness, and/or to place students in homogenously tracked classes. Still other schools may be seeking special funding available to schools whose students excel on the exams.

CONCERNS ABOUT STANDARDIZED TESTS

PARENTS and educators have three main objections to standardized tests: first, that classroom curriculum gets short-changed in an effort to "teach to the test"; second, that the assumption behind standardized tests—that students can be assessed equally with one test—is inherently flawed; and third, that teacher and school bonuses and funding should not be determined by standardized test results.

Teaching to the Test

A growing concern among parents and teachers is how high-stakes testing affects the classroom. On the one hand, as one middle school principal says, "Of course the tests are important. But if you have strong curriculum that is well designed, the tests are three or four days of lost time, and not much more." In other words, if your eighth grader's school has designed its curriculum to meet state content standards, you probably don't have much to worry about in this category. But this assumes that the standardized test *also* tests to those specific state content standards, and that might not be the case in your state. Many states administer one of five "generic" tests commonly used across the country: the California Achievement Tests, the Comprehensive Tests of Basic Skills (CTBS), the Iowa Tests of Basic Skills (ITBS), and the Stanford Achievement Tests (SAT). If these tests don't specifically match the state's content—or if your teen's curriculum doesn't quite match state standards—he and his classmates may "lose" three or four weeks of class time preparing for the exam. That's why a growing number of states, such as Pennsylvania, Texas, and Florida, have commissioned their own proprietary standardized tests.

Whether your state uses a generic or proprietary test, it remains up to each school to determine *how* to meet the state content standards in the classroom, and different schools may have very different approaches that meet with different levels of success. Standardized tests therefore remain an important way to measure whether individual schools and districts are giving students the knowledge and skills state educators have deemed necessary for that grade level. Still, if your teen's teachers need more than a week to help students prepare for standardized tests, you may want to find out why the district is instituting the exams and why students need special preparation for the tests.

Measuring Achievement

Despite the excessive attention politicians and the media often pay to test scores, it's important to remember that no standardized test purports to be an accurate measure of the whole child, and educators and administrators are well aware that many factors affect student performance on standardized tests. Poor performance may in fact have little to do with a student's aptitude or the efficacy of her teachers. A number of important studies have shown a strong correlation between economic status and standardized test scores: the higher the economic status of the area, the higher the overall test scores. This may be caused by a lower quality of school buildings and materials, less money for teacher training and extracurricular and parent-involvement programs, and environmental stresses in poorer areas. Of course, this remains a generalization, and there are often remarkable exceptions—a stellar school in a poverty-stricken district, for example. The same is true on the individual level as well. Wealthier students don't always perform better on exams, and a number of important factors—including motivation, stress, and illness—can have a tremendous impact on a student's test scores.

Standardized test scores, therefore, should be taken with the proverbial grain of salt. They're only one indication of skill and achievement. Grades, portfolios, and teacher evaluations give a much more complete picture of a student's true achievement and aptitude. Despite political pressure to the contrary, then, standardized tests should be seen as only a benchmarking tool, not as an absolute measure of a student's performance or potential.

> I do agree that one test offers very little information. You need multiple tests to . . . draw valid conclusions. I do agree with that. But I'm concerned a little about the negative tone that tests have generated across the country. And the purpose of the test is not to deny people things or to bring about negative impact. The purpose of the testing is to determine whether or not we've been effective in whatever efforts and methods that we're using.
>
> —ROD PAIGE, U.S. SECRETARY OF EDUCATION, ONLINE NEWSHOUR INTERVIEW, JANUARY 10, 2001.

Test Scores Tied to Punishment or Reward

One of the more heated debates now is about the use of test scores to punish or reward individual teachers and schools. California's new Academic Performance Indicator initiative, for example, actually rewards teachers and schools financially with "bonuses" based on test scores. Bush's proposal sets up bonus funds for outstanding schools and threatens to cut funding for those that "fail to make adequate yearly progress for their disadvantaged students."

Parents and students worry that such programs will encourage teachers to "teach to the test" or encourage administrators to put more pressure on teachers to "teach to the test," with the result that test preparation will seriously cut into class time. In addition, because in some states individuals can earn financial bonuses for high test scores, some fear that monetary rewards to teachers and schools may even induce less scrupulous teachers or administrators to tamper with test results.

Ironically, this trend, which has so many parents up in arms, has come about largely in response to parental demand for greater accountability in schools. But it is a practice that must be managed carefully. After all, just as standardized test results are only one measure of an individual student, they are only *one* measure of the success of a particular teacher or a school.

DEALING WITH STANDARDIZED TESTS

DESPITE these valid concerns, standardized tests are here, and it looks like they are here to stay. If you feel that standardized tests are so problematic that they should be dramatically revamped or even abolished, then you may choose to become politically involved, like the boycotting parents in Scarsdale. If you recognize the value of standardized tests as *one* evaluative tool, however, and you wish to support your teen as he takes these exams, there are many sensible steps you can take to help him do well.

Learn About the Test

Perhaps the most important thing you can do to help your teen is to be informed. At the beginning of the school year, speak with a school teacher or administrator to obtain the following information:

➤ Which test(s) will be administered during the school year?
➤ When will those tests be administered?
➤ Why does the school administer this test? For what purpose(s)?
➤ What material will be covered, and in what format? (For example, multiple choice only, multiple choice and essay?)
➤ How much class time will be devoted to preparation for the test?
➤ Will the school provide test-taking practice, or is that something you should provide?

➤ How will your teen's teachers and the school use the results of the test? For example, will the test scores determine your teen's placement in certain classes next year?

➤ What other means of evaluation will the teachers and school use to measure your teen's performance?

After you've received your teen's test results, you may want to follow up with these important questions:

➤ How did students in your teen's school compare with students in other school systems across the state or country (depending upon the type of exam)?

➤ What do the test results indicate regarding your teen's skills and abilities?

➤ Are the test results consistent with your teen's performance in the classroom?

➤ Based on the test results, are there any changes anticipated in your teen's educational program?

➤ Is there anything you can do at home to help your teen strengthen particular skills?

Help Your Teen Prepare

In addition, there are several things you can do to help your teen be well prepared for standardized tests when they roll around. Whether or not your school considers standardized tests "high stakes" or "just another test," you can help your teen do well by having the right attitude and teaching effective test-taking strategies throughout the year. Here are some specific suggestions:

Keep the pressure to a minimum. A little nervousness can be a good thing, but test anxiety can spell disaster, even for the best of students. Students who experience test anxiety are afraid of failure and extremely self-critical. They feel that *they*, and not their learning or achievement, is what is being tested—that is, if they fail a test, *they* are a failure. Test anxiety is often rooted in parental pressure. If you put too much pressure on your teen to perform, she might be so afraid of failing that she'll make errors on questions that she can normally handle.

Under Pressure

It's important to remember that even if parents aren't directly "pressuring" their teen for high test scores, in today's competitive school environment, teens may be placing undo pressure on themselves. When asked about what kinds of fears or pressure he faces this year as an eighth grader, Andrew from suburban New York said that he was worried not about school violence, making the baseball team, or peer pressure to drink, but about the new assessment and exit exams in the works for New York state. His parents and teachers were surprised by his answer.

Help your teen practice effective test preparation. As you should for any test, teach your teen to space out studying over several days or weeks prior to the exam so that your teen can adequately address any problem areas and review all of the material more than once to feel sufficiently prepared. (Putting all tests and assignment due dates on a calendar is your best bet.) Don't let your teen "cram" the night before. Cramming only increases anxiety, which in turn will inhibit your teen's ability to think clearly. It will also prevent your teen from getting a good night's sleep, which is essential.

Teach your teen the importance of reading directions carefully before beginning an exam or assignment. Misunderstood directions can mean disastrous results on your teen's test. Make sure your teen knows to ask for clarification if she does not understand the directions clearly.

Instructions Are Important

Is your teen good at following directions? If not, she could be in big trouble when she takes a standardized test. Here's a quick exercise to help your teen realize the importance of following directions carefully:

1. Read all directions before you begin.
2. Write your full name in all capital letters in the space below.
3. Use the letters in your name to create three words of at least three letters each. Write those words below.
4. Count the number of letters in your full name. Write that number below.
5. Subtract your age from the number of letters in your name.
6. After you've read the directions, ignore all other instructions and simply sign your name in the space below.

Review multiple-choice and timed-test strategies. On a timed test, it's important to answer as many questions as possible. Let your teen know that if she gets stuck on an answer, she should skip it and go on to the next one. If she has time left at the end of the exam, she can go back and answer the questions she left blank.

For standardized tests, find out if your student will *lose* points for incorrectly answered questions or if her score will be based only on the number of questions she answers correctly. If she will lose full credit for incorrect answers, she should leave all unanswered questions blank at the end. However, if she has nothing to lose by answering a question incorrectly, she should take as many educated guesses as possible and then simply answer the remaining blank questions randomly. If she will lose a fraction of a point for an incorrect answer, she should see if she can eliminate one or more possible answers. If so, she'll greatly increase the odds of answering correctly. For example, if there are four possible answers and she can eliminate two, she has a 50-50 chance of earning a full credit, and a 50-50 chance of losing $\frac{1}{4}$ of a point if she is wrong. It would be to her advantage to then take an educated guess at the answer.

Make regular attendance a priority. Standardized tests are designed to measure achievement through the school year, so it's important that your teen be in class, learning the required material every day, unless he is ill or has a family emergency.

Pay attention to bodily needs. Your teen's physical state will affect his mental abilities. If he's feeling run-down, for example, he won't be able to think as quickly or make connections as easily. On each school day, and especially on test days, help your teen get to bed early enough to get a good night's sleep and prepare a nutritious breakfast the next morning. A well-rested and well-fed student will usually fare far better than one who is sleepy or hungry, and unable to concentrate.

Ten Things You Can Do to Help Your Teen Succeed on Standardized Tests

1. **Know what test and when.** Find out at the beginning of the school year which test(s) your teen will be taking and when. Know exactly what subjects will be covered, how the test will be formatted, and how the results will be used.

2. **Help your teen identify weaknesses.** Once you know what will be covered on the test, sit down with your teen and review those subject areas. Are there any areas in which your teen needs real improvement? Ask the appropriate teacher for specific suggestions about how your teen can best prepare for the upcoming test.

3. **Review the format and rules.** Your teen should have taken standardized tests at least once by now, but that doesn't mean he's comfortable with the standardized test structure, and it may have been four years since his last standardized test. It may help if you explain why the test environment is so demanding and why the rules must be strictly followed. After all, the results of a standardized test can only be *standard* to the extent that all test-takers and administrators follow precisely the same procedures.

4. **Boost confidence.** Self-esteem is an important factor in test success. Make a habit of praising your teen for work well done and make sure that your praise is specific.

5. **Have realistic expectations.** Expecting too much from your teen can be as damaging as expecting too little and may create debilitating test anxiety for your teen.

6. **Remember that this is only one test.** Make sure your teen understands that this is only one of many measures of her academic abilities and only one small judgment of her academic success. Your teen will keep the results in proper perspective only if you do, so you, too, must avoid blowing the test and test results out of proportion.

7. **Set up a test-prep study schedule.** A few weeks before the test, create a special study schedule for your teen to review the material that will be tested. This could be just 15 minutes a day. This short review will help your teen feel more comfortable and prepared.

8. **Get test accessories ready.** Take a small load off your teen by taking care of the little details. Make sure your teen has everything he needs for the test the night before. Collect any necessary accessories such as #2 pencils, erasers, and a calculator, if permitted.

9. **Bed and breakfast.** A good night's sleep is extremely important; your teen will have difficulty performing to the best of her ability if she's tired. Likewise, make sure she fuels up with a nutritious breakfast (see page 68) to give her energy for the exam.

10. **Keep cool.** Relax. If you're frantic, you'll only make your teen more nervous than necessary. Once again, it's only one test. Set a good example for your teen by staying calm and keeping things in perspective.

SAMPLE QUESTIONS

TO give you a sense of the kind of questions your eighth grader will face on standardized tests this year, the following section contains a few sample questions from typical eighth grade reading and math exams.

Reading Comprehension

Eighth grade reading tests typically consist of several reading passages of up to two pages in length. They are followed by multiple-choice or written response questions that usually cover the following areas:

➤ vocabulary (questions usually test the ability to determine meaning from context, but some will test general word knowledge)
➤ identifying the main idea
➤ specific facts and details
➤ ability to draw logical inferences from the evidence in the story
➤ recognizing organizational patterns and writing strategies
➤ distinguishing fact from opinion
➤ interpreting visual information

The reading passages will cover many genres, including fiction, poetry, narrative, and expository prose, such as argumentative essays, excerpts from textbooks or newspaper articles.

SAMPLE 1

A Day at the Nature Center

Emma stared sadly out the window of the bus. The farm was only fifty miles outside of town. She thought about the farm all the time, remembering the breathtaking view from her bedroom window, the creaky wooden floors of the old farmhouse, and especially the animals.

When Emma's parents sold their hundred-acre farm and moved to the nearby town of Carrville, Emma had been enthusiastic. But when she got to the new school, she felt overwhelmingly shy around so many strangers.

With a sigh, Emma turned her attention back to the present. The bus came to a stop, and Emma climbed off with the rest of her Earth Studies classmates. "Welcome to the Leinweber Nature Center," her teacher, Mrs. Bowes, announced. "In a few minutes, a guide will give us a presentation about the area's native animals and habitat. After the presentation, you'll have a worksheet to complete while you explore the rest of the center. Now, I want everyone to find a partner."

Emma looked around apprehensively as her classmates began to pair up. She didn't have any friends yet—who would be her partner? Emma hesitated for a moment and then approached Julia, a talkative and outgoing girl who sat near her in class. "Could I be your partner?" Emma asked tentatively.

"Sure," said Julia warmly. "Let's go get the worksheet from Mrs. Bowes."

Together, the girls walked into the Leinweber Nature Center. They listened to the guide talk about how the workers at the center cared for injured and orphaned animals and how the center tried to recreate the animals' natural habitats as much as possible. Emma listened intently. She thought it would be wonderful to have a job that involved nurturing and caring for animals all day.

After the presentation, the girls examined their worksheets. "Let's see," said Julia, "One of the things we're supposed to do is locate the rodent area and assist with feeding the baby squirrels. How big is a baby squirrel? Do you think we actually have to hold one? Maybe you should let me feed it while you watch." Julia was so excited that she fired off one question after another and didn't wait for a response from Emma.

Emma and Julia walked into the rodent area and stood there, looking around at all of the rats, mice, chipmunks, and squirrels. "Hi there!" boomed an enthusiastic voice from behind them. "I'm Josh Headly, the keeper in charge of rodents. Did you come to see the squirrels?"

"Yes," said Emma, turning around with an eager smile on her face. "Do we actually get to feed the babies?"

"You sure do. Here—let me demonstrate the feeding procedure for you."

Josh showed them how to wrap a baby squirrel in a towel and hold the bottle of warm milk. Emma settled back into a chair, enjoying the warmth of the tiny ball of fur nestled in her hand. She flashed a smile over at Julia, but Julia, who was suddenly silent, was focusing on her own baby squirrel.

After the babies were finished eating, Josh asked, "Would you like to help feed the adult squirrels, too?"

Emma was quick to volunteer, but when Josh opened the first cage, the squirrel inside leaped out. Julia shrieked and tried to jump out of the way. Emma, who maintained her composure, bent down, held out her hand, and made quiet, soothing sounds. The runaway squirrel cocked its head to one side and seemed to listen to her. Quickly, while the squirrel was distracted by Emma, Josh reached over and scooped it up.

He smiled appreciatively. "Good job, Emma! It's not easy to remain calm when a wild animal gets out of its cage. I'm impressed!"

"Wow!" Julia chimed in. "You're always so quiet. I thought you were shy and scared of everything, but you're braver than I am if you can get close to a wild animal, even if it is just a squirrel."

"I'm only shy around people, not animals. And I used to live on a farm, so I know that when animals are scared or excited, you have to stay calm—even when you don't feel calm—if you want to help them."

Josh nodded in agreement. "You know," he began, "we've been taking applications for part-time volunteers to help out with the animals. Would you be interested in interviewing for a volunteer position here at the center?"

"Interested? I would love to work here! What an opportunity! Where are the application forms? When could I start?" Now it was Emma who was so excited she couldn't wait for a response.

That afternoon, in the bus on the way back to school, Emma sat next to Julia. A rush of newfound contentedness washed over her. Not only had she found a place full of animals to help take care of, but she had also made a new friend.

Questions

1. In which of the following ways are Emma and Julia **alike**?
a. They both are very outgoing and talkative.
b. They both feel comfortable around animals.
c. They both have a class called Earth Studies.
d. They both live on farms outside of Carrville.

2. Which words best describe how Emma feels when her class-mates first begin to pair up?
a. angry and disappointed
b. anxious and uncertain
c. enthusiastic and joyful
d. jealous and hurt

3. Re-read the following sentence from the story:

Emma hesitated for a moment and then approached Julia, a talkative and outgoing girl who sat near her in class. "Could I be your part-ner?" Emma asked tentatively.

As it is used in the story, what does the word *tentatively* mean?
a. carelessly
b. eagerly
c. forcefully
d. cautiously

4. The author presents Julia as someone who
a. makes friends easily.
b. is fun-loving but a poor student.
c. knows a lot about animals.
d. treats her friends badly.

5. Arrange the following events in the order that they took place in the story:
1. Julia and Emma sat together on the bus.
2. A guide spoke about the nature center.

3. Emma and Julia fed some baby squirrels.

4. Josh introduced himself to the two girls.

   a. 3, 4, 2, 1

   b. 2, 4, 3, 1

   c. 1, 2, 4, 3

   d. 1, 4, 3, 2

6. Which word best describes Julia's tone in the following paragraph?

"Wow!" Julia chimed in. "You're always so quiet. I thought you were shy and scared of everything, but you're braver than I am if you can get close to a wild animal, even if it is just a squirrel."

   a. impressed

   b. jealous

   c. disbelieving

   d. embarrassed

7. Re-read Emma's reaction to Josh's offer below

"Interested? I would love to work here! What an opportunity! Where are the application forms? When could I start?"

The style of Emma's response

   a. helps create an excited tone.

   b. is repetitive and dull.

   c. shows that she is unsure about what to do.

   d. reflects her shy nature.

8. Emma is happy at the end of the story because

   a. she is no longer shy.

   b. she will be paid well for her work at the nature center.

   c. she has a new job and a new friend.

   d. she thinks Josh has a crush on her.

Answers

1. c
2. b
3. d
4. a
5. b
6. a
7. a
8. c

SAMPLE 2

Treating Burns

There are three different kinds of burns: first degree, second degree, and third degree. Each type of burn requires a different type of medical treatment.

The least serious burn is the first degree burn. This burn causes the skin to turn red but does not cause blistering. A mild sunburn is a good example of a first degree burn, and, like a mild sunburn, first degree burns generally do not require medical treatment other than a gentle cooling of the burned skin with ice or cold tap water.

Second degree burns, on the other hand, do cause blistering of the skin and should be treated immediately. These burns should be immersed in warm water and then wrapped in a sterile dressing or bandage. (Do not apply butter or grease to these burns. Despite the old wives' tale, butter does not help burns heal and actually increases the chances of infection.) If a second degree burn covers a large part of the body, then the victim should be taken to the hospital immediately for medical care.

Third degree burns are those that char the skin and turn it black or burn so deeply that the skin shows white. These burns usually result from direct contact with flames and have a great chance of becoming infected. All third degree burn victims should receive immediate hospital care. Burns should not be immersed in water, and charred clothing should not be removed from the victim as it may also remove the skin. If possible, a sterile dressing or bandage should be applied to burns before the victim is transported to the hospital.

Questions

1. The main idea of this passage is best expressed in which sentence?
   a. Third degree burns are very serious.
   b. There are three different kinds of burns.
   c. Some burns require medical treatment.
   d. Each type of burn requires a different type of treatment.

2. This passage uses which of the following patterns of organization?
   a. cause and effect, comparison and contrast, and order of importance
   b. cause and effect, chronology, and order of importance
   c. comparison and contrast only
   d. cause and effect and comparison and contrast only

3. A mild sunburn should be treated by
   a. removing charred clothing.
   b. immersing it in warm water and wrapping it in a sterile bandage.
   c. getting immediate medical attention.
   d. gently cooling the burned skin with cool water.

4. This passage uses the third person point of view because
   a. the author wants to create a personal and friendly tone.
   b. the author wants to present important information objectively.
   c. the author wants to put readers in his shoes.
   d. the author does not have a specific audience.

Answers

1. d
2. c
3. d
4. b

Math

Math tests will typically cover basic math skills and number knowledge, graphic representations and equations, geometry, basic algebra, and probability and statistics.

1. Alexandra made two candles, one in the shape of a cylinder and the other in the shape of a triangular prism. How much more wax did she use for the cylindrical candle? (Use π = 3.14.) Record your answer on the grid in the answer book.

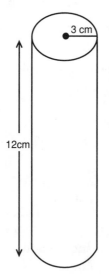 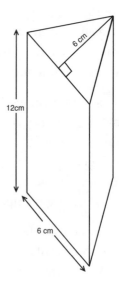

2. Five years ago, the animal shelter organized an annual bicycle race to raise funds for a vaccination program. Participation increased steadily every year, as shown in the table below.

YEAR	# OF CYCLISTS
1	684
2	931
3	1176
4	1412
5	1859

Part A—Make scatter plot of the data. Use the space provided in the answer book.

Part B—If the participation continues to increase at a similar rate, about how many cyclists will participate in the sixth year of the race. Estimate your answer, and explain how you determined your estimate. Use the space provided in the answer book.

3. An airplane departs Kennedy Airport at 3:18 P.M. and arrives in Buffalo at 5:04 P.M. What was the duration of the flight?

a. 1 hour, 44 minutes

b. 1 hour, 46 minutes

c. 2 hours, 4 minutes

d. 2 hours, 26 minutes

4. Joe and Bob have part time jobs, and work on afternoons and on weekends. Joe works 18 hours a week, which is four more than twice as many hours as Bob works. If B stands for the number of hours Bob works, which of the equations below could be used to find the value of B?

a. $18 = 4 + 2B$

b. $2 \times 18 = 4 + B$

c. $18 + 4 = 2B$

d. $\frac{1}{2}(18) = 4 + B$

5. The admission fee for the high school play was $2.50 for parents and $1.10 for students. After the play, the student council counted the money and found that they had collected $1060.80 in admission fees.

Part A—If 401 parents attended the play, write an equation that could be used to solve for s, the number of students who attended the play.

Equation: _____

Part B—Solve the equation that you wrote to determine the number of students who attended the play.

Show your work:

STANDARDIZED TESTS BY STATE

Standardized testing is always changing. At the time of publication, the information listed below was current and accurate. It is important to contact your child's school early in the year to confirm what tests are going to be given, what topics will be covered, and when the tests will be given.

States that require standardized testing in eighth grade include:

State:	**Alaska**
Name of Test:	Alaska Benchmark Examination
Subjects Tested:	Reading, Writing, Mathematics
Month Given:	March

State:	**Arizona**
Name of Test:	Stanford Achievement Test 9th Edition (SAT 9)
Subjects Tested:	Reading, Mathematics, Language
Month Given:	March, April

State:	**California**
Name of Test:	Stanford Achievement Test, 9th Edition (SAT 9)
Subjects Tested:	Reading, Writing, Spelling, Mathematics
Month Given:	March, April

State:	**Colorado**
Name of Test:	Colorado Student Assessment Program (CSAP)
Subjects Tested:	Reading, Mathematics, Science
Month Given:	March, April

State:	**Connecticut**
Name of Test:	Connecticut Mastery Test
Subjects Tested:	Reading, Writing, Mathematics
Month Given:	March, April

State:	**Delaware**
Name of Test:	Delaware Student Testing Program (DSTP)
Subjects Tested:	Reading, Writing, Mathematics, Science, Social Studies
Month Given:	April, May

State: **Florida**
Name of Test: Florida Comprehensive Assessment Test (FCAT)
Subjects Tested: Reading, Mathematics
Month Given: February, March

State: **Georgia**
Name of Test: Norm-referenced Tests (NRT), Criterion-referenced Competency Tests (CRCT)
Subjects Tested: Reading, Writing, Mathematics, Science, Social Studies
Month Given: March, April, May

State: **Illinois**
Name of Test: Illinois Standards Achievement Test (ISAT)
Subjects Tested: Reading, Writing, Mathematics
Month Given: April

State: **Indiana**
Name of Test: Indiana Statewide Testing for Educational Progress (ISTEP+)
Subjects Tested: Mathematics, Reading, Language Arts
Month Given: September, October

State: **Iowa**
Name of Test: Iowa Test of Basic Skills (ITBS)
Subjects Tested: Reading, Writing, Mathematics
Month Given: N/A

State: **Kansas**
Name of Test: Kansas Assessment Program (KAP)
Subjects Tested: Reading, Writing, Mathematics, Social Studies
Month Given: March, April

State: **Kentucky**
Name of Test: Kentucky Core Content Tests
Subjects Tested: Mathematics, Social Studies, Arts, Humanities, Practical Living/Vocational Studies
Month Given: April, May

State: **Louisiana**
Name of Test: Louisiana Educational Assessment Program for the 21st Century (LEAP 21)
Subjects Tested: English Language Arts, Mathematics, Science, Social Studies
Month Given: February, March

State: **Maine**
Name of Test: Maine Educational Assessment (MEA)
Subjects Tested: Reading, Writing, Health, Mathematics, Social Studies, Science, Fine Arts
Month Given: March/November/December

State: **Maryland**
Name of Test: Maryland School Performance Assessment Program (MSPAP)
Subjects Tested: Reading, Writing, Language Arts, Mathematics, Science, Social Studies
Month Given: April, May

State: **Massachusetts**
Name of Test: Massachusetts Comprehensive Assessment System (MCAS)
Subjects Tested: English Language Arts, Mathematics, Science & Technology, History and Social Science
Month Given: March, April

State: **Michigan**
Name of Test: Michigan Educational Assessment Program
Subjects Tested: Science, Writing, Social Studies
Month Given: N/A

State: **Minnesota**
Name of Test: Basic Standards Test (BST)
Subjects Tested: Reading, Mathematics
Month Given: February

State: **Missouri**
Name of Test: Missouri Assessment Program (MAP)
Subjects Tested: Mathematics, Language Arts, Fine Arts, Social Studies, Science, Health
Month Given: March, April

State: **Montana**
Name of Test: N/A
Subjects Tested: Reading, Communication Arts, Mathematics, Science, Social Studies
Month Given: April, May

State: Nevada
Name of Test: Nevada Writing Assessment Program/ Terra Nova
Subjects Tested: Writing/ Reading, Language Arts, Mathematics, Science
Month Given: N/A

State: New Jersey
Name of Test: Grade Eight Proficiency Exam (GEPA)
Subjects Tested: Reading, Writing, Mathematics, Science, Social Studies, Fine Arts (Health and World Languages will be added in 2002–2003 and 2003–2004 respectively.)
Month Given: March

State: New York
Name of Test: New York 8th Grade Assessments
Subjects Tested: English Language Arts, Mathematics/ Science, Social Studies
Month Given: January, February/May, June

State: North Carolina
Name of Test: 8th Grade End-of-Grade Tests
Subjects Tested: Reading, Writing, Mathematics
Month Given: May, June

State: North Dakota
Name of Test: Test of Cognitive Skills, 2nd Edition (TCS/2), Terra Nova
Subjects Tested: Reading, Language Arts, Mathematics, Spelling, Science, Social Studies
Month Given: N/A

State: Oklahoma
Name of Test: Oklahoma Core Curriculum Tests (OCCT)
Subjects Tested: Reading, Writing, Mathematics, Science, History, Geography, The Arts
Month Given: March, April

State: Oregon
Name of Test: Oregon Statewide Assessment, Benchmark 3
Subjects Tested: Writing, Reading/Literature, Mathematics, Science, Extended Career and Life Role Assessment
Month Given: January, February, March, April

State:	**Pennsylvania**
Name of Test:	Pennsylvania System of School Assessment (PSSA)
Subjects Tested:	Reading, Mathematics
Month Given:	N/A

State:	**Rhode Island**
Name of Test:	*New Standards* Mathematics Reference Exam, *New Standards* English Language Arts Reference Exam, National Assessment of Educational Progress (NAEP)
Subjects Tested:	Mathematics, English Language Arts, Reading, Science, History, The Arts
Month Given:	N/A

State:	**South Carolina**
Name of Test:	Palmetto Achievement Challenge Test (PACT)
Subjects Tested:	Language Arts, Mathematics, (Science to be added in 2002)
Month Given:	April, May

State:	**Tennessee**
Name of Test:	Tennessee Comprehensive Assessment Program (TCAP)
Subjects Tested:	Reading, Language Arts, Mathematics, Science, and Social Studies
Month Given:	March, April

State:	**Texas**
Name of Test:	Texas Assessment of Academic Skills (TAAS)
Subjects Tested:	Reading, Writing, Mathematics, Science, Social Studies
Month Given:	March, April

State:	**Utah**
Name of Test:	Stanford Achievement Test, 9th Edition (SAT 9)
Subjects Tested:	Reading, Language Arts, Mathematics
Month Given:	N/A

State:	**Vermont**
Name of Test:	New Standards Reference Exam, Written Language Portfolio, Mathematics Problem Solving and Communication Portfolio
Subjects Tested:	English/Language Arts, Mathematics, Writing
Month Given:	N/A

State: **Virginia**
Name of Test: Standards of Learning Assessment (SOL)
Subjects Tested: English, Mathematics, History, Social Science, Science
Month Given: October, March

State: **Washington**
Name of Test: Washington Assessment of Student Learning (WASL)
Subjects Tested: Science
Month Given: April, May

State: **Wisconsin**
Name of Test: Wisconsin Knowledge and Concepts Examinations (WKCE)
Subjects Tested: Reading, Language Arts, Writing, Mathematics, Science, Social Studies
Month Given: February

State: **Wyoming**
Name of Test: Wyoming Comprehensive Assessment System (WyCAS)
Subjects Tested: Reading, Writing, Mathematics
Month Given: April

SUMMARY

AS controversial as they may be, standardized tests are used in schools across the country, and it soon may be a federal requirement to test students every year from the third through eighth grades. Most states currently test eighth graders in reading and math, and these test results may be used for grade promotion and tracking of individual students, school and/or teacher rewards, and overall school and program assessment. Find out exactly what tests your teen will be expected to take and why. Know when the tests will be administered and how the school will help your teen prepare—or whether test prep is entirely up to you and your teen. Be sure to keep the pressure to a minimum, for test anxiety can cripple your teen at test time. Remember that standardized tests are only one measure of your teen's academic achievement.

chapter 6

Your Child's Social and Emotional Development

AUTHOR'S NOTE: This chapter was written in consultation with Dr. Timothy Dunnigan, a clinical psychologist and family therapist in San Diego, California. Dr. Dunnigan is the author of *HELP for Families* and www.helpforfamilies.com.

"I used to be my child's best friend, a regular hero," says Carl, father of an eighth grade boy. "But these days, everything I say and do is stupid, my son is embarrassed to be seen with me, and he's convinced that I can't possibly understand what he's going through."

Trish, mother of three, reports, "All of my children changed dramatically around the eighth grade. They'd all been so well behaved—never talked back, never challenged my authority. Then in middle school something happened. They couldn't stand to be told what to do."

"I don't know what to do with my daughter," worries Carol, mother of an eighth grader. "She has the most incredible mood swings! One

minute she's her normal, cheerful self, and the next she's running up to her room in tears—and I have no idea what happened."

Sound familiar? If so, take heart—for these are all typical eighth grade behaviors. But just because they're typical doesn't mean they will be easy to handle. No matter how close a relationship you may have with your child, eighth grade is likely to be a challenging year for both of you.

Socially and emotionally, your eighth grader will undergo many important changes this year. Adolescents spend a great deal of emotional energy struggling to establish their own identity. They distance themselves from their parents in an effort to become an individual, yet at the same time their sense of self is shaped largely by the opinions of their peers. As adolescents hit puberty, they become increasingly self-conscious and worry intensely about their appearance and behavior; they rebel against authority as they seek more control over their lives. They're caught between childhood and adulthood—too old for dolls but too young to date; too old to play with cars but too young to drive.

Your role as a parent and your relationship with your child will change as well during this turbulent time. You will need to learn to communicate with your adolescent in different ways; you will need to find the right balance between holding tight and letting go; and you will need to stand by a teen who is constantly pushing you away but who still desperately wants your approval and needs your support. That support begins with understanding just what's going on developmentally with your child.

THE MIND-BODY CONNECTION

THE turmoil of the eighth grade year has its roots in a powerful combination of physical and intellectual changes taking place in your child. Your teen is developing tremendous new cognitive abilities, the most significant being the ability to think abstractly. This means that not only can your adolescent think symbolically—an essential skill for the eighth grade curriculum and beyond—but also that your teen is beginning to understand important abstract concepts such as love, justice, and honor. (This does not mean that your teen is suddenly able to have a mature love relationship with a peer, but it does mean that your teen will be deeply involved in exploring this emotion.)

Hand in hand with this cognitive leap is the ability to approach subjects and situations systematically and to envision hypothetical situations. This means your adolescent is now capable of carefully thinking through "what if" scenarios and imagining possible outcomes. He'll also be spending a lot more time thinking about the future—about dating and driving, for example, and college and careers.

Physically, your teen is developing an adult body, which means she will have to take on adult responsibilities for that body—even though she's still an adolescent. Boys will confront new challenges, too, particularly in learning how to handle their emotions, which they will often be expected to hide. They will face lots of pressure to act tough and will frequently worry that they aren't "manly" enough, especially if they're among the shortest in the class.

Because of intense hormonal activity, your teen may also experience dramatic mood swings and periods of extreme sensitivity. A minor incident such as an inability to find a favorite sweater or baseball cap may result in a disproportionate emotional outpour. These hormonal changes combined with social and academic pressures may disrupt adolescent sleep patterns, and they may develop new (usually less healthy) eating habits, which in turn will further increase their moodiness and sensitivity. Hormones may also trouble self-conscious teens with acne, and rapid and uneven growth may make them feel awkward and even more insecure.

Indeed, your emotionally vulnerable teen is likely to be painfully conscious of every imperfection. Because adolescents are changing so rapidly, they're very preoccupied with those changes and understandably worry about how those changes will affect their relationships with others (especially their peers). And because they're so self-conscious, most adolescents feel that others are preoccupied with them as well, and your teen may imagine that other people are always looking at him and judging him. Meanwhile, because they're not yet comfortable with their new bodies and evolving personalities, adolescents tend to be extremely self-critical. A minor problem such as a facial blemish may create intense embarrassment for your teen, who fears others may reject him because of his imperfections.

A new body, a new way of understanding the world . . . your teen is indeed becoming a new person. He just hasn't quite figured out who that person is yet.

A NEW IDENTITY

PERHAPS the most important and most difficult aspect of an adolescent's journey is his struggle to establish his own identity. Eighth graders are learning who they are and who they want to be, and to develop their individuality and independence, they need to break free from their parents and make more and more decisions on their own. They want to grow up fast, and they want the adults in their lives to acknowledge their maturity.

But of course adolescents *are* adolescents—they're not yet adults, despite what their bodies and the media lead them to believe. They are not mature enough or emotionally experienced enough to make important decisions about their future, about their bodies, and about peer relationships without your guidance.

Bullies, Geeks, and Jocks: Fitting In and Feeling Left Out

Because they are just starting on the long journey of self-discovery, and because they are now developing strong romantic feelings for their peers—whose approval they desire as much as, if not more than, their parents'—adolescents tend to use the acceptance of their peers as the primary measure of their self-worth. Even teens who had a strong self-esteem prior to adolescence often will become remarkably insecure around the eighth grade and will constantly seek approval from peers.

Of course, this need to be accepted by peers creates a problematic middle school environment that can lead to counter-productive behavior. Everyone desperately wants to belong—and at this age, conformity to group standards often means that teens who did not have high self-esteem prior to adolescence suppress the selves they really want to be in order to fit in. In middle school, like it or not, just about everyone gets labeled as a "jock," "brain," "geek," "loser," or some other stereotype. If it's a negative label, teens will often try to fight it, and therefore not be true to themselves (for example, a student may deliberately do poorly on schoolwork if he is being ridiculed for being a "brain"). And teens may go through erratic stages when they try to be someone they're not in order to attain a desired label or join the "in" crowd.

Experimentation

Fortunately for adolescents, *everyone* is going through these changes, and there's an aura of "temporary-ness" in middle schools that gives teens the freedom to experiment with different "versions" of themselves. Eighth graders will typically experiment in one or more of the following areas:

Activities, hobbies, and clubs

Each of us has a distinct combination of interests and talents that helps to distinguish us as a unique individual. Identifying and exploring these interests and talents is critical in developing and maintaining a healthy self-esteem. The extracurricular activities offered at most middle schools are therefore very important for adolescents, who may try their hand at several different clubs and sports throughout their middle school years. Your teen may be surprised by how much she enjoys an activity she had never tried before or how little she likes an activity she thought she'd enjoy, and your teen's activities can help her discover talents she didn't know she had. (For more information about extracurricular activities, see Chapter 3.)

Friends and social groups

Eighth graders typically form very close friendships as they seek more and more support and companionship from their peers. Your teen will likely have one or two "best friends" with whom she may exchange phone calls or e-mails several times a day (even after passing notes or sending messages all day long at school). Strong as these friendships may be, though, they can also be very fickle, and they can end over seemingly trivial incidents. Don't be surprised if your teen suddenly drops his long-time pal in favor of someone new. As teens find out more and more about themselves, they may seek out others who share more of their interests. And, unfortunately many teens will end good friendships in an attempt to move up the school social ladder and join a more "in" clique.

Style

Right or wrong, a major factor determining whether or not your teen will fit in is his appearance. Facial or physical features matter, but more important to his peers will be your adolescent's style (clothes, hair style, jewelry, and make-up). Certain looks are "in," others are definitely "out"—and if your teen sports an outdated style, he can probably expect to face intense ridicule from his peers. Don't be too surprised if your son suddenly trades in his preppy clothes for over-sized t-shirts, baggy jeans, and a beaded choker or if your daughter won't leave the house without a mesh bag and platform shoes.

In addition to the normal cultural pressure to be "in style," your teen may feel added pressure to look a certain way because that is the dress code of a particular social group at school. And while your teen's obsession with clothes (and frequent changes in style) may frustrate you, remember that he believes (and his peers reinforce this belief) that there's an awful lot at stake here. Remember, that as long as you are paying for the clothes that your teen wears, you have a say in what they wear. Keeping your teen in the latest style can get expensive, and the latest style, for example midriff-baring shirts, may not be what you want to see your teen in. Have your say in how you spend your money.

Because style is an important way of expressing one's self (and children recognize this fact rather early on), adolescents begin to consciously use clothing (and make-up, hair styles, and jewelry) as a way of asserting their individuality. Of course, in most cases, they're not adopting a truly unique style but choosing, from the array of styles available, the style that they feel best expresses who they are (or who they want to be). Still, your teen's style can help him feel more comfortable with his developing identity. For example, if your teen always wears a certain kind of hat or always styles her hair in a particular (and unusual) way, and this style is accepted by her peers, it can have a tremendous impact on her self-esteem.

Not Music to Your Ears?

Though many parents of today's eighth graders grew up on rock-'n-roll, there's still a good chance that your teen's musical tastes will differ greatly from yours. This is to be expected; after all, your teen is trying to build a separate identity and wants to listen to a musical style of his own. It's especially important, therefore, not to be critical of your teen's musical preferences *unless* the music promotes hateful or self-destructive behavior. Here are a few tips for a more harmonious household:

- ❐ Know what your teen is listening to. Learn the names of his favorite bands and find out a bit about their background. Make it a point to read the lyrics of some of the songs—but don't march into his room and demand the CD. Instead, try a softer approach: "I hear the songs that you're playing but I can't understand what the singer is saying. Mind if I look at the liner notes?" These words express your interest and concern, not a desire to control what he listens to.
- ❐ If you discover that the lyrics of your teen's favorite songs are violent or hateful, discuss them with your teen immediately. It is possible that your son or daughter doesn't quite understand the full meaning of the words. If she does understand the lyrics, explain why they concern you and how you feel about her listening to that kind of music.
- ❐ Ask your teen what she likes about the music she's listening to. How does it make her feel? Why? Talk about

why you like your favorite bands and performers and how they make you feel.

❑ Share with your teen the music you listened to as an adolescent and talk about why it was important to you. Your teen might think you corny or old-fashioned, but it will help your adolescent a great deal to have you share these important emotions. Even though your teen may remain convinced that "you just don't understand," you can still attempt to show that you do.

❑ Unless your child has an allowance that gives him the freedom to purchase music on his own, understand you have the right as a parent to question what music your teen listens to before he buys it.

Music

Music is extremely important for adolescents, who, because of their inexperience with the complex emotions they are beginning to feel, often believe that no one understands what they are going through. But music can often speak to teens in a way that adults and even their peers can't, and when your teen finds music that helps him express his emotions, he's likely to become a very passionate fan. Don't be surprised if you hear the same album (or even the same song) played over, and over, and over again as your teen revels in music that gives him both pleasure and comfort.

Musical taste, like style, is an important aspect of our individuality, and you can expect your teen to "try on" many different musical styles (such as hip-hop, punk, rap, hard rock, rhythm and blues) until he finds a style that "fits" his tastes (and meets with the approval of his peers). Remember that musical styles also have corresponding lifestyles and dress codes. If your teen goes through a heavy metal music phase, for example, don't be surprised if he starts to dress accordingly in black T-shirts, torn jeans, and studded jewelry. (And don't forget the unkempt hair.)

The music that moves your teen will probably *not* be the music you'd prefer to hear, but this is only normal. Chances are that your parents didn't like the music you listened to as a teen, either. It's important for teens to establish a musical identity that's different from their parents' (just like they will want to dress differently from you, too). If you're particularly displeased with your teen's favorite bands, take heart. It's likely that your teen will shift loyalties as the tastes of his peer groups change, and as he gets older, he'll become more discriminating in his musical tastes.

A Healthy Obsession?

Your teen's room is plastered with pictures of Tiger Woods. Newspaper and magazine articles, posters, and advertisements cover the walls. Your son watches every tournament in which Tiger plays, has read every word ever written about the golf star, and even has his own Tiger Woods webpage. Is this normal? Is this okay? Yes, and yes—that is, as long as the person or group your teen worships is a positive role model. And Tiger Woods certainly fits that bill.

Other celebrities, however, may not be so good for your adolescent's character development. A performer such as Britney Spears, for example, may inspire your teen to join the choir or dance club at school, but someone like Spears may also encourage your adolescent to exploit the sexuality she's only just beginning to learn how to handle. If you're worried that your child's object of obsession is problematic, make sure you discuss your concerns in a *non-judgmental* manner. Explain honestly why you're worried about this person as a role model for your teen.

Of course, a *true* obsession can be dangerous. If your child's interest in an athlete, entertainer, or possibly even a classmate seems excessive—that is, if it seems to be disrupting his normal routine or interfering with his schoolwork and relationships—then you may have a more serious problem on your hands. In that case, it's best to seek some professional advice on how to help your child.

Alcohol and Drugs

As much as you might wish you could, you can't hide drugs and alcohol from your child. They're everywhere in our culture, and frightening as it may be, most teens will experiment with drinking and/or drugs in high school—and maybe even earlier. And the younger a child is when he first tries alcohol, the more likely he is to experiment with more dangerous drugs as a teen.

Sobering Statistics

According to the 1998 Washington State Survey of Adolescent Health Behaviors, 31% of eighth graders surveyed had consumed alcohol within the past 30 days; 15% had smoked cigarettes; and 16.5% had smoked marijuana.

According to the organization Mothers Against Drunk Driving, a study of ninth graders from four urban high schools showed that the best predictor of risky sexual behavior was alcohol and/or drug use.

There are many reasons why even "good" kids who should know better experiment with these substances. For one thing, teens expect it to be fun; because of how drugs and alcohol are portrayed in the media, and especially because of the way drinking is associated with celebration, teens expect to have a good time. Adolescents may also experiment with these substances because it helps them feel more in control—they're making an important (though unwise) decision about their bodies on their own. Further, experimentation often helps teens fit in—peer pressure to drink or do drugs can be extremely strong, even as early as the eighth grade. In addition, teens may use alcohol or drugs to escape from the social, emotional, or academic pressure they face at school or at home.

Sexual Activity

Even more frightening, perhaps, is the fact that your eighth grader may start experimenting with sexual behaviors. Like alcohol and drugs, sex is everywhere in our culture, especially in advertisements and on TV. Adolescents with particularly low esteem are especially vulnerable to early experimentation with sex, for they are more likely to confuse sex with love and to therefore engage in sexual activity to feel some measure of self-worth. Peer pressure to be sexually active can also be very strong in the eighth grade. Experimenting with sex may also be important to a teen who is unclear about his sexual orientation and is seeking some clarification.

❏ It is estimated that more than 15 million new cases of sexually transmitted infections (STIs) are diagnosed each year in the United States (Cates, 1999)– Approximately one-fourth of these new infections occur among teenagers (Center for Disease Control, 2000).

❏ In the United States, 47% of teens say they personally need more information on how to prevent AIDS and other STIs.

❏ The average age of first intercourse in the United States is 16, and 66% of high school seniors have intercourse before they graduate.

❏ One million American teenagers become pregnant each year. The majority of these pregnancies–78%–are unintended (AGI, 1999).

Source: Planned Parenthood® Federation of America, Inc. Copyright © 1998, 2000, 2001.

CHALLENGING AUTHORITY

BECAUSE adolescents are now officially on their way to being grown-ups, they begin to look at grown-ups very differently. "Who are these people trying to control me," they wonder, "and what gives them the right to tell me what to do?" They begin to realize that adults aren't perfect, and they will look for your faults (and perhaps even point them out to you repeatedly). This is partly a result of their insecurity (they tend to see themselves as greatly flawed, and it gives them a small feeling of power to be able to find fault in you, too) and partly due to their need to try to gain a more equal footing with adults. They will question and challenge authority—yours, teachers', indeed any adult's—because *they* want to be the ones making decisions about what they should or should not do.

BATTLING BULLIES

MOST teens are lucky enough to escape the wrath of the inevitable class bully. But someone ends up bearing the brunt of that bully's anger—and what if that someone is your child?

If your teen is the victim of verbal or physical abuse from classmates, for your child's sake and the sake of the bully and other potential victims, take action. Though bullying is common in the eighth grade, victims are often told to simply ignore the bully on the assumption that the bullying will stop. But if little or no action is taken against the bully, whether or not the bully continues to pick on the same child, the bully and his classmates will get the message that his behavior is acceptable.

Indeed, in recent studies of bullying behavior, researchers repeatedly found that witnesses to a bullying session will usually either watch silently (thus signifying approval) or chant encouragement. Very few witnesses will get help or intervene in an attempt to stop the bullying because they're afraid of being the next victim or of being labeled a "tattle tale" by their classmates. Some researchers also believe that bullying is generally accepted at this age because of an underlying belief that bullying helps "toughen up" the "weaklings."

But this of course is not always—or even usually—the case, and the acceptance of bullying behavior sends a very negative message about our values. *No one* deserves to be threatened or physically violated on any level, and letting bullies get away with their behavior teaches students that some people don't deserve respect. It also encourages the bully's violent behavior and may lead him to commit increasingly violent acts as well as entice others to enter the bullying ring.

To protect your child, find out whether your teen's school has a policy regarding bullying behavior. If not, demand that one be developed. Your teen's schools should be a place where *each* child is treated with equal respect, and students should know that the verbal or physical abuse of classmates will result in significant penalties for the offenders. Be sure that your teen's school's teachers and administrators fully support the policy and follow through with penalties. If not, don't hesitate to take the matter to the school board.

HELPING YOUR TEEN THROUGH TRYING TIMES

YOUR eighth grader will face lots of challenges this year, and there are certain to be rough times ahead. But you can do a great deal to lessen the turmoil while at the same time building your teen's esteem and character.

Stay Involved

Once again, perhaps the most important thing you can do is to stay involved. Know what's going on in your teen's life. Who are his friends? What's happening in school? What are his strengths and weaknesses? What gets him upset? What makes him proud? How does he like to spend his time? What music does he listen to? What shows does he like to watch on TV? Who has he chosen as a role model? Who is his current crush?

If you don't know the answers to these questions, ask. And never hesitate to ask your teen about where he's going and what he plans to do. At this age, it's extremely important for you to keep tabs on your teen. Watch for signs of maladjustment or drug use and talk with your teen immediately if you suspect a problem.

A Different Perspective

You know what your teen is like at home, but what's your teen like at school? It's possible that your teen behaves very differently in the classroom and hallways at school. To get a better picture of your child's social development, ask your child's teachers the following questions the next time you meet (or, if you think you have reason to worry, call and schedule a conference with your teen's teachers or guidance counselor now):

1. What does my child seem to like best in school?
2. What seems to be the area he/she enjoys least?
3. Does he/she seem to be doing his/her best, putting forth a good effort?
4. How does my teen seem to be doing with other kids? Does he/she seem to have a group of good friends? Does he/she seem to fit in?
5. Is there anything my teen does that seems to make social relationships difficult? Does he/she pick on others—or is he/she being picked upon by others? If so, does he/she seem to do anything to encourage this behavior?
6. Have you seen any warning signs or changes in behavior that we should check into?
7. What are my teen's best and worst subjects?
8. How does my teen participate in class? Does he/she seem too shy, or perhaps too vocal? Does he/she tend to encourage classmates? Cooperate well with others?
9. What are the social issues in the classroom? How can I help my teen deal with them at home?

SOURCE: ADAPTED FROM HOME AND SCHOOL INSTITUTE (HSI), COPYRIGHT © 1989. SEE ALSO *MEGASKILLS: BUILDING ACHIEVEMENT FOR THE INFORMATION AGE* BY DOROTHY RICH (HOUGHTON MIFFLIN, 1998).

Talk with Your Teen

"I try to talk to my teen, but I can't seem to get a conversation going," many eighth grade parents report. Effective communication is a challenge, and it's especially challenging with an adolescent. Of course, that only makes effective communication all the more important. You need to be able to clearly express your expectations and concerns and discuss issues that matter with your teen.

To help you get your teen talking, and to get your teen to listen to what you have to say, use the following guidelines:

➤ **Be honest and open.** When talking with your teen, always be honest and open. Honesty conveys a respect for and trust in your teen, and your willingness to share your feelings accomplishes two very important goals: First, it shows your teen that it's okay to express emotions even though this makes us vulnerable. Second, by showing that you can be vulnerable, too, you build trust with your teen, who will be more confident that you will respect his emotions and not take advantage of his vulnerability.

➤ **Talk about important issues early and regularly.** Even if you're uncomfortable—in fact, *especially* if you're uncomfortable—start talking, and keep talking, about issues that are important to you and your teen, including sexual activity and drug use. Don't wait until your teen comes to you about these issues. If you don't bring up these subjects, chances are that your teen will think she can't talk to you about these issues, so she may not come to you at all—or may only come when it's already too late.

You may not feel like your talks have any effect, but just the fact that you are addressing these issues will make your teen aware that they're very serious matters and that you are willing to talk about them. Your effort *will* be appreciated, because it shows that you care about the conflicts your teen will face and how your teen will handle them. Besides, if you don't talk with your teen about sex, drugs, and alcohol, someone else *will*.

Beyond the Birds and the Bees

A recent survey conducted by the Kaiser Family Foundation, Children Now, and Nickelodeon found that many parents are putting off talking about tough issues like sex and puberty with their kids. More than half of parents of teens 12–15 have not talked with their child about how to know when they are ready to have sex, and a quarter haven't talked about puberty or the basics of reproduction.

But many teens want to hear from their parents. Nearly half of all 12–15 year olds said they wanted to know *more* about the following issues:

❐ how to protect themselves against HIV/AIDS
❐ how to handle the pressure to have sex
❐ how to know when they are ready to have sex

SOURCE: "TALKING WITH KIDS ABOUT TOUGH ISSUES:
A NATIONAL SURVEY OF PARENTS AND KIDS." MARCH, 2001.
KAISER FAMILY FOUNDATION, NICKELODEON, AND CHILDREN NOW.

I had to put aside my own embarrrassment to talk to my son about sex. I admit it was awkward at first, but then I realized how important it was. He had plenty of questions and I was happy to be giving him the answers instead of him getting information, or even worse, misinformation, from his friends or others. It wasn't easy, but it was the best thing I could have done for him.

—A PARENT FROM SAN DIEGO, CALIFORNIA

Use "I-talk"

Because teens are so sensitive, it's especially important to avoid openly judging or criticizing your child, which will only put her on the defensive and encourage her to shut you out. Instead, use non-judgmental, honest, "I-talk"—a strategy that locates the "problem" with you, not your teen, and focuses on the emotions you're feeling. For example, if your normally chatty teen has been unusually quiet recently, you might actually *prevent* communication and anger your teen by saying, "What's wrong with you? Why are you so quiet?" The language here directs everything at your teen and doesn't reflect that you are concerned about her sudden silence. "I-talk," on the other hand, stresses your concern for your teen's welfare and her relationships with you and others. Here's how you might approach the same problem with "I-talk":

> *"I've noticed that you've been much quieter than usual lately. I'm used to you being much more talkative. Is everything all right? Would you like to talk?"*

Even if your teen declines your invitation, you've helped a great deal by showing that you care and that you aren't judging her or criticizing her for her behavior. Here's another example. Imagine that your teen's room is a disaster—again. You might be tempted to say something like, "Your room is such a mess! Why can't you keep your room clean?" That approach pretty much guarantees a defensive or rebellious response. "I-talk", on the other hand, actually communicates what you *really* are feeling:

> *"I don't like to see your room such a mess. It makes me angry to see your things all over the floor when I work hard to keep the rest of the house clean. I'd really like you to pick up your clothes."*

"I-talk" is also a great conversation starter. Instead of trying to get a discussion going with, "So, what would you do if someone asked you to try drugs?" try an "I-talk" approach:

> *"I was thinking about you today, and I was wondering what you'd do if someone offered you drugs."*

Listen to Your Teen

Communication is a two-way street. When one person is talking, the other person needs to be listening—and both people need to have the opportunity to express their feelings. Here are some strategies for effective listening:

➤ **Paraphrase** what your teen tells you to be sure you understand what he's saying. All too often people don't say exactly what they mean, especially when they're not sure how to explain what they feel or when they're afraid of being criticized or judged. And just as often, people hear what they *want* to hear and not what is actually being said. That's why it's crucial that you get in the habit of paraphrasing when you talk with your teen. In your own words, express what you believe your teen is saying. Your teen can then confirm that you understand him correctly or help you see how he really feels. Here's an example:

> Teen: I don't want to take piano lessons anymore. I don't like playing the piano.
>
> Parent: You're not enjoying the lessons anymore and you want to quit, huh?
>
> Teen: Yeah. I mean, they used to be fun and all, but not anymore.
>
> Parent: Something's changed.
>
> Teen: Yeah . . . .The lessons are too hard for me now, you know? I'm just not that good at the piano and all I get is frustrated now. It's not fun anymore. I don't want to go because I know I'll feel stupid and keep screwing up.

Notice how the parent's responses acknowledged the teen's feelings, which in turn encouraged the teen to explain why she felt that way.

➤ **Let your teen talk.** In James Baldwin's powerful short story "Sonny's Blues" (1948), Sonny tries to talk with his older brother about his passion for jazz music and his desire to escape the drug culture of their neighborhood in Harlem. But it's a one-way conversation, because Sonny's brother isn't listening. "I hear you," Sonny tells his brother, "But you never hear anything *I* say." When your teen talks with you, give her your complete attention and resist the urge to interrupt, except to paraphrase. Don't preach. *Listen.*

➤ **Acknowledge your teen's feelings.** Try as you may, you might not be able to convince your teen that you *do* understand what she's going through or convince her that her friends are not always talking about her behind her back. But that's okay. What's important is that you *acknowledge* her feelings. Denying a child's emotions at any age can cause critical damage to her self-esteem, causing her to think she's not normal or that there's something wrong with *her* and not others. Even if you can't fix the problem—and so many adolescent concerns are problems that they need to work through themselves—you can bring your child great comfort by showing that you are aware of how she feels. This can give her the support she needs to work things through. For example, if your teen has had a fight with her best friend, a simple "I can see that you're really angry with Chris. It looks like she hurt you pretty badly" will validate your teen's emotions, strengthen her sense of self, and possibly encourage her to share her feelings with you in more detail.

➤ **What not to do**: Never tell your teen that he shouldn't be feeling the way he does. "Don't be so upset; it's just one pimple" will only make things worse because your teen will feel that you're dismissing his feelings. Instead, acknowledge your adolescent's insecurity: "You think it looks pretty bad, and you're worried that people will make fun of you, aren't you?" This will help him accept his emotions and manage them more effectively.

➤ **Pay attention to silences** and what your teen does not say. If it's been a few weeks since your child has mentioned anything about her favorite club or it's been days since you've heard anything about her best friend, it could be a sign that something happened or that something's troubling your teen. Use these silences to open discussions. Try "I-talk" to get things started: "I've been wondering about Jennelle. I haven't heard you mention her in a while" or "I was hoping to see the new project you're working on for your photography club. I really like what you did last time. What are you working on now?"

Set Clear Rules and Restrictions on Behavior and Consequences for Breaking Those Rules

Being involved also means establishing and enforcing rules. Adolescents are not adults yet, and they still need clear guidelines about what is and isn't permissible behavior. You must be absolutely clear about the big issues including sex, drugs, and violence, but you should also be clear about rules and expectations regarding regular "everyday" activities and behaviors such as homework, household chores, and the respectful treatment of others.

It's equally important to be clear about the specific penalties for breaking these rules and enforce those penalties. Be fair and consistent in establishing and enforcing punishments. Be sure to follow through; if you don't, you can expect future infractions. Allow your teen to have a say in determining rules and punishments, too; this demonstrates a healthy respect for his ability to distinguish right from wrong and helps develop his sense of fairness and responsibility. And remember that as angry as your teen may be about being punished, on one level (which he probably doesn't even realize), he's probably a little bit glad. Rules, regulations, and appropriate punishments help children of all ages feel loved and secure.

Warning Signs

With all the physical, emotional, and behavioral changes that teens experience, how do you know what's "normal" and what's a sign of trouble? While some withdrawal and aggression is normal at this age, **excessive aggression or withdrawal** is a sign that your teen is not coping well with her emotional and physical changes. An emotionally healthy teen should continue to treat family members respectfully and continue to earn grades consistent with her past abilities. If your teen has trouble meeting these expectations, or if you notice excessive withdrawal or aggression, try making your expectations more clear to your teen and make a strong effort to more openly acknowledge your teen's emotions. If you don't see improvement within a few days, your teen may need some professional support.

Encourage Character Development

Never underestimate your power as a role model. To help your teen develop socially, emotionally, and morally, model good behavior. Be honest and fair, respect others at all times, act responsibly, and demonstrate your trustworthiness. By modeling good behavior, you can help your teen build up the strength to make difficult decisions and give him specific strategies for handling sticky situations. For example, if someone with whom you don't want to speak calls on the phone, don't ask your teen to lie and say that you're not home. Instead, take the call and deal with the situation. This approach will teach your teen to face responsibilities, even if they're unpleasant, and it demonstrates respect for others.

Respect Your Teen's Developing Self

Finally, it's absolutely essential to respect your teen in all of the various stages of developing self-hood. Specifically:

➤ **Give your teen the freedom to be an adolescent.** Allow her to express those emotional ups and downs. Don't demand that she be happy; let her express her feelings and learn how to deal with the wide range of emotions she'll be feeling. This may mean that you'll have to give *yourself* more freedom to be an emotional parent. "Parents who understand their own emotions and are secure with them are best able to cope with their children's moodiness," says Dr. Timothy Dunnigan, a clinical psychologist and family therapist. "Insecure parents often feel that it is a negative reflection on them that their child is feeling down. Parents who are not secure with anger or sadness or boredom, which are legitimate experiences, may struggle to have their child act happy, despite what real problem the child may be experiencing. This denies the child the learning that comes from being able to express the feelings one is having, understand why one is experiencing those feelings, and put the feelings in perspective with the rest of one's life."

➤ **Praise plentifully.** Help your teen fight the insecurity of adolescence by providing plenty of specific praise. Find several things to praise her for each day. Remember, the more specific, the better. A quick "Hey, you chose a nice outfit today" can help your teen feel good throughout the day (even if she thinks you don't know the first thing about style). Also, notice this comment praises her for her decision and not for her clothes.

➤ **Give age-appropriate freedoms** to teach responsibility and demonstrate your trust and respect for your teen. This, of course, is one of the most difficult aspects of parenting a teen. How much freedom is enough to teach him self-reliance and responsibility while still keeping him safe from behaviors or situations that can hurt him? The answer isn't clear, for each teen is different and lives in unique circumstances. But it *is* clear that you have to do some letting go. If you try to control too many aspects of your teen's life, you will find your child rebelling wildly and making poor choices, putting himself (and perhaps others) at great risk. Your teen will also take longer to develop good decision-making skills if you don't allow him to start making more decisions on his own.

How much freedom is appropriate for eighth graders? By age 10–11, you and your teen should each be making about 50% of the decisions in your child's daily life. As your teen gets older, the balance should shift, little by little, until your teen, at 18, is making just about all of his decisions for himself. *Which* decisions should be left to your teen at age 13 is another issue. Some things seem quite clear: your teen should be able to choose the extracurricular activities in which he wants to be involved (finances permitting), for example, and your teen should have the freedom to choose his friends—though again you have the right to step in if your teen gets in with a dangerous crowd.

There are also many small but important decisions you can hand over to your teen, such as which chores he'd like to do around the house (maybe he'd rather do laundry than vacuum) or what to eat for lunch on a Saturday. You can also provide many limited freedoms that can help your teen develop decision-making skills while staying within certain boundaries. For example, you could allow your teen to pick out her back-to-school wardrobe entirely on her own, with three exceptions: no bare midriffs, no offensive decals, and no high heels.

She'll deeply appreciate your trust in her judgment, and chances are you'll be more pleased by her choices than you might have expected.

SUMMARY

HOW much your teen will change this year! As bodies begin to mature, your teen may become surprisingly moody and sensitive, and he may seem as if he's obsessed with the changes taking place in his body. He'll begin to think abstractly and hypothetically, and he'll spend a lot of time thinking about the future. As he begins to establish a separate identity, he may push you away and resist your control while looking more and more to his peers for acceptance. He'll spend a lot of time experimenting with different activities, friends, styles, and music, and he may even try alcohol, drugs, or some sexual activity.

To support your teen as he undergoes these profound changes and to help him become a strong person who makes wise decisions, *stay involved*. Talk with your teen, listen actively and carefully, set clear rules and consequences for breaking those rules, encourage character development, and at all times *respect* your teen.

chapter 7

Looking Ahead: College Bound and Other Choices

AUTHOR'S NOTE: This chapter was written in consultation with Barbara Lyon, an 8th grade guidance counselor in Alpharetta, Georgia.

PERHAPS when your child was four, he wanted to be a firefighter; at five, a police officer; at six, an astronaut; at seven, a doctor. Now, at 13 or 14, he may be thinking more seriously about the future, but he still seems to change his mind about careers every couple of months, and you're sure he'll change his mind another four dozen times before he even graduates from middle school. So what's the sense of talking to him seriously about career options at this age?

Actually, adolescence is the ideal time to lay the foundation of vocational identity, for your teen is already very busy thinking about herself and her future, exploring her interests, skills and aptitudes, and experimenting with adult roles. Career education complements these developmental activities and supports your teen's academic and emotional development by encouraging her to think critically, expand her horizons, develop her strengths, and improve her weaknesses.

In the past, opponents of career education in the middle school argued that adolescents are too early in the identity formation stage for vocational instruction and that career education at this age tends to push students into career tracks too early, cutting them off from other options. But research in the last decade has found strong evidence that career education in the middle school is necessary. Consider the following facts:

➤ By adolescence, most middle schoolers have already accepted sex-role stereotypes (e.g., that only girls can be nurses or that only boys should be scientists).

➤ Students with low self-esteem assume their career options are limited.

➤ Most middle schoolers are unrealistic about career plans and do not realize that school performance and class choices today can limit or expand future opportunities.

➤ Most adolescents have a limited understanding of the social value of work and of the diversity of occupations.

Today's middle school career education programs have therefore been designed to accomplish some very specific goals:

1. To help students better understand themselves by clearly identifying their interests, skills, and aptitudes.

2. To help students develop tentative career goals based on those interests, skills, and aptitudes.

3. To help students eliminate career-related stereotypes and to consider more career options.

4. To help students understand the social value of work and respect workers of all kinds.

5. To introduce students to a broad range of careers and discuss the various paths for career preparation.

Career education typically takes place through workshops or special career education courses taught by guidance counselors or interdisciplinary faculty teams. In addition, in most middle schools, vocational education also occurs regularly across the curriculum. For example, in a science class, students may be asked to write report on a career in science. In computer class, students may learn how to format documents by developing a resume. Meanwhile, in English, students may discuss techniques for creating a persuasive cover letter and address grammatical issues by carefully proofreading their resume.

But adolescent career education at the middle school is carefully limited. After all, eighth graders are still just learning how to think abstractly and explore possibilities for their future in a meaningful way. And educators are well aware that it's dangerous to push adolescents, who are still in early stages of identity formation, to make firm career choices so early. Thus, career education for eighth graders remains exploratory in nature and focuses on understanding the self and the nature and value of life work.

The new trends in middle school career education have had a noticeable impact, especially in recent years with the wealth of career and college information available online through the Internet. Barbara Lyon, an eighth grade guidance counselor at Taylor Road Middle School in Alpharetta, Georgia, notes that when she became a counselor over a decade ago, 90% of the eighth graders she surveyed said they wanted to be "singers or dancers or baseball stars." Now, through Taylor Road's career education program, which includes lots of time exploring careers online in the computer lab, adolescents are becoming much more realistic about future careers and are becoming interested in a greater variety of career options. Though it's still common for adolescents to want to be famous performers or professional athletes, more and more eighth graders are citing career interests such as marine biology, aerospace engineering, and physical therapy.

YOUR ROLE AS A CAREER COUNSELOR

As the person who knows your child best, there's a great deal you can do to supplement the career education taking place in your teen's school. Here are five specific things you can do to help:

1. Discuss various career and college options with your teen.
2. Help your teen identify his interests, strengths, and aptitudes.
3. Help your teen gain exposure to various occupations.
4. Work with your teen's guidance counselor.
5. Be open and supportive about career interests.

DISCUSS CAREER AND COLLEGE OPTIONS

WHATEVER your teen's tentative plans post-graduation, chances are her knowledge of career and college options is limited. To make the right choice, your teen needs to make a fully-informed choice, and she should be aware of these options.

Two- and Four-Year Colleges

When we hear the word "college," we typically think of the kind that offers a four-year program leading to a Bachelor of Arts (BA) or Bachelor of Science (BS) degree—the kind of school your child should attend if he wants to go to medical school or law school, become a teacher or social worker, or learn how to guide a rocket or create a complicated computer program. A BS or BA degree is required for any advanced or professional degree program, including:

➤ DDS—Doctor of Dental Surgery
➤ JD—Juris Doctor
➤ MA—Master of Arts
➤ MBA—Master of Business Administration
➤ MD— Doctor of Medicine
➤ MFA—Master of Fine Arts
➤ MPhil—Master of Philosophy
➤ MS—Master of Science
➤ PhD—Doctor of Philosophy

Depending upon your teen's academic abilities and career goals, a two-year college may be a more viable option. Two-year colleges offer an associate's degree which can lead to many different careers, including the following:

➤ computer support specialists
➤ paralegals and legal assistants
➤ physical therapy assistants
➤ medical records and health information technicians
➤ respiratory therapists
➤ dental hygienists
➤ occupational therapy assistants
➤ cardiovascular technologists and technicians

Many graduates of two-year colleges later transfer to four-year schools and earn a higher degree.

Specialized Post-Secondary Schools

In addition to two- and four-year schools, there are hundreds of specialized post-secondary schools across the country, some of which offer associate's or bachelor's degrees, others of which offer professional certification. The curriculum at most of these schools still includes the basics (such as courses in communication and the appropriate math and sciences), but the coursework focuses on a specific skill or trade, such as carpentry, cooking, or computer repair. Here's a sampling of the kinds of trade or specialized schools available:

➤ acupuncture
➤ art/design
➤ automotive repair
➤ barbering/hair stylist
➤ bartending
➤ cosmetology
➤ computers/technology
➤ culinary
➤ electronics
➤ flying

➤ gemology
➤ health services (technicians, assistants, aides)
➤ plumbing
➤ telecommunications
➤ travel
➤ welding

What's Hot

The Bureau of Labor Statistics (BLS) cites the following jobs as the **ten fastest-growing occupations** in the United States through 2008. Note the varying levels of education and training required for these positions:

Rank	Occupation	% Increase	Education/Training
1	Computer engineers	108	Bachelor's degree
2	Computer support specialists	102	Associate's degree
3	Systems analysts	94	Bachelor's degree
4	Database administrators	77	Bachelor's degree
5	Desktop publishing specialists	73	Long-term on-the-job training
6	Paralegals and legal assistants	62	Associate's degree
7	Personal care and home health aides	58	Short-term on-the-job training
8	Medical assistants	58	Moderate-term on-the-job training
9	Social and human service assistants	53	Moderate-term on-the-job training
10	Physician assistants	48	Bachelor's degree

Several of these jobs are also among the occupations with the **largest projected job growth** for the 1998–2008 period:

	Job Title	Projected # of New Jobs
1	Systems analysts	577,000
2	Retail salespersons	563,000
3	Cashiers	556,000
4	General managers and top executives	551,000
5	Truck drivers, light and heavy	493,000
6	Office clerks, general	463,000
7	Registered nurses	451,000
8	Computer support specialists	439,000
9	Personal care and home health aides	433,000
10	Teacher assistants	375,000

Finally, here's the BLS's list of the ten industries with the **fastest wage and salary employment growth** for 1998–2008:

Industry	Employment Change			
	1998	**2008**	**Number**	**Percent**
Computer and data processing services	1,599,000	3,472,000	1,872,000	117
Health services, not elsewhere classified	1,209	2,018	809	67
Residential care	747	1,171	424	57
Management and public relations	1,034	1,500	466	45
Personnel supply services	3,230	4,623	1,393	43
Miscellaneous equipment rental and leasing	258	369	111	43
Museums, botanical and zoological gardens	93	131	39	42
Research and testing services	614	861	247	40
Miscellaneous transportation services	236	329	94	40
Security and commodity brokers	645	900	255	40

FOR MORE INFORMATION, VISIT THE BUREAU OF LABOR STATISTICS ONLINE AT WWW.BLS.GOV/OCOHOME.HTM.

The Military

Another viable option for many students is to enter one of the five service branches of the military: the Army, Navy, Air Force, Marine Corps, and Coast Guard. The U.S. Government hires approximately 365,000 new enlisted and officer personnel each year and offers over 10,000 courses in over 300 schools to its employees free of charge, allowing military personnel the opportunity to earn a college degree while they train and work. Though many of us tend to think of combat when we think of the military, the service branches offer thousands of jobs in non-combat categories, including:

➤ human services
➤ media/public affairs
➤ healthcare
➤ engineering, science, and technology
➤ administration
➤ electronics
➤ construction
➤ machinery operation, maintenance, and repair
➤ transportation

Of course, the military requires employees to commit to a certain period of service, and membership in the military entails the risk of serving in a combat zone in the event of a war.

The Work Force

There are many reasons teens consider entering the work force right after high school. Perhaps they've already found a rewarding career through part-time work or an apprenticeship in school. Perhaps they're just not sure what they want to do and hope a year or two in the "real world" can help them decide on what type of schooling to pursue. Perhaps there are economic or family considerations, such as the need to take care of an ailing family member. Or perhaps they're rebelling against family or societal pressure to go to college.

If your child is seriously considering entering the workforce, then it's your job to help him carefully examine his reasons for rejecting or postponing post-secondary education. While there is always the risk that your teen won't go back to school if he decides to postpone college, there are many students for whom a year or two of work is a valuable learning experience that enables them to be more focused and apply themselves more successfully when they do go back to school.

By taking time off, for example, your teen might quickly realize that she needs more education to do the kind of work—or earn the kind of pay—that she'll find satisfying. Consider the following statistics gathered by the Bureau of Labor Statistics:

Unemployment and Earnings for Year-Round, Full-Time Workers Age 25 and Over, by Educational Attainment

Unemployment rate in 1998 (Percent)	Education attained	Median earnings in 1997 (dollars)
1.3	Professional degree	72,700
1.4	Doctorate	62,400
1.6	Master's degree	50,000
1.9	Bachelor's degree	40,100
2.5	Associate's degree	31,700
3.2	Some college, no degree	30,400
4.0	High-school graduate	26,000
7.1	Less than a high-school diploma	19,700

As this table clearly shows, there's a strong correlation between level of education and employability—the higher your degree, the less likely you are to be unemployed. And, the higher your level of education, the higher the salary you're likely to earn. It's not impossible for a high school graduate with no further education to earn a six-figure income, of course, but that kind of salary is much more realistic for someone who's earned a professional degree.

Remember, too, that your child doesn't have to go to school full-time. Your teen could start working while he takes a few introductory college courses. By the time he has to declare a major, he will already have significant work experience under his belt and hopefully a much clearer understanding of his career goals.

Unusual Careers

Is your teen the type who likes to do things out of the ordinary? Perhaps she'd be interested in one of these more unusual careers:

- ❏ Aquarium or zoo keeper
- ❏ Arborist (tree care specialist)
- ❏ Body parts model
- ❏ Book cover designer
- ❏ Comedian
- ❏ Conference planner
- ❏ Demolitions expert
- ❏ Dog trainer
- ❏ Fishing boat captain
- ❏ Food stylist (photography)
- ❏ High-rise window washer
- ❏ Hotel service evaluator
- ❏ Juvenile fiction writer
- ❏ Ice sculpture carver
- ❏ Industry inspector
- ❏ Massage therapist
- ❏ Package designer
- ❏ Product tester
- ❏ Restaurant reviewer
- ❏ Secret shopper or store detective
- ❏ Sound effects specialist
- ❏ Speech writer
- ❏ Taxidermist
- ❏ Technical translator
- ❏ Website monitor

HELP YOUR TEEN IDENTIFY INTERESTS, SKILLS, AND APTITUDES

IF your teen is to find a career that is both emotionally and financially rewarding, she'll need to find a career that suits her personality and abilities. A square peg won't fit into a round hole, and if your teen ends up in a career that she doesn't enjoy, it will have a negative impact on all areas of her life. To get on the right career track, your teen needs to have a better understanding of herself, and you can assist your teen by helping her identify her interests. What does she like to do? Why? Have your teen make a list of things that she enjoys and explain why she enjoys them. Then, help your teen identify her skills and aptitudes. What is she good at? What are her strengths and weaknesses? Again, have her make a list. You and your teen can revisit these lists over the next few years as your teen continues her academic, social, and emotional development, and as she identifies more specific career goals, she can determine which weaknesses, if any, need to be improved for her to reach those goals.

For example, if your teen, who is an excellent artist, is interested in a career in graphic design but has very little computer experience, he will need to take computer courses, join a technology club, and/or learn desktop publishing software at home on his own in order to make graphic design a viable career goal. First, however, he may want to do extensive research in graphic design careers and get a rough measure of his aptitude for computers. Your teen's guidance counselor can provide him with various aptitude "tests" to help him determine his academic, artistic, and mechanical strengths and weaknesses. A number of helpful aptitude tests are also available online at sites like www.stanfordplus.com/education/test/aptitude.php and www.target-future.org/NewFiles/car-aptitude.html.

HELP YOUR TEEN LEARN ABOUT VARIOUS OCCUPATIONS

WHEN it comes to thinking about careers, eighth graders are still in a bit of a dream world. But that's probably a good thing, because it means that your eighth grader is still unfocused enough to be willing to consider a tremendous range of job possibilities.

You might want to begin by showing your teen the following list of job categories. What areas seem to interest him right off the bat? Then, see if he can name specific job titles for each category (a list of examples is located at the end of this chapter). Help your teen add to this list. Now that he sees a variety of specific job titles, do other job categories grab his interest? Are there specific areas he'd like to explore?

General Career Categories:
> ➤ administrative/support
> ➤ arts/design
> ➤ business/finance
> ➤ communications
> ➤ computers/technology
> ➤ education
> ➤ environmental
> ➤ healthcare/medical
> ➤ hospitality
> ➤ legal
> ➤ performance
> ➤ public service
> ➤ retail
> ➤ science/engineering
> ➤ social services
> ➤ trade/manufacturing

Like your teen's lists of strengths, weaknesses, and interests, this is a list he can come back to, perhaps several times a year, as he develops a better understanding of himself and his career goals.

Bring your teen to work with you and arrange for her to visit other workplaces. Help your teen become more realistic about the world of work by bringing her along for a day of work. Let her see what you do and what others in your workplace do. Arrange for her to "shadow" several of your coworkers so that she can observe many different jobs within your organization. See if she can do the same with a relative or close friend so she can visit several workplaces in this manner.

Help arrange volunteer opportunities or internships for your child. Your teen can gain invaluable career perspective by working as a volunteer or, when he's older, a paid intern at a nursing home, hospital, television or radio station, law office, or local museum, for example. Help your teen find volunteer organizations in his areas of interest. For example, Emmanuel, an eighth grader from Iowa City, had always loved animals, and he found a volunteer opportunity with a local animal shelter. Twice a week, he grooms and feeds abused and abandoned pets while he learns more about animal care and the workings of a nonprofit organization.

Explore careers and schools on the Web with your teen. There are many excellent career-oriented websites that can help your teen identify interests and learn more about specific careers. Some particularly helpful sites include:

- ➤ www.collegeboard.com On this site, the College Board offers advice about planning a career, choosing a college, and tackling college admission tests. It also offers detailed job descriptions for dozens of job titles. You can also download a free multimedia program called GrO—Going Right On—designed especially for middle schoolers to start thinking about college.
- ➤ www.bls.gov The Bureau of Labor Statistics offers a wide variety of career information, including statistics on job growth and earnings and detailed job descriptions.
- ➤ www.acinet.org/acinet/ America's Career Info Net lists wage and employment trends, education and training requirements for numerous careers, labor market conditions, and an extensive career resource library.

➤ **www.ams.org/careers/** This Mathematical Sciences Career Association site describes various non-academic jobs in industry and government for mathematicians.

➤ **www.jobprofiles.com/** JobProfiles.com offers career descriptions with a focus on the personal side of work. The site is designed particularly for students and aims to help students find a good match between their interests and skills and a career.

➤ **www.militarycareers.com** This military career site describes hundreds of military careers and related benefits such as free college tuition.

WORK WITH YOUR TEEN'S GUIDANCE COUNSELOR

EVERY middle school has at least one guidance counselor, and usually at least one guidance counselor specifically assigned to each grade. Guidance counselors typically serve three main functions: to counsel students who have personal, family, or academic problems; to guide students in career education; and to help students develop and maintain strong study skills.

While your teen won't see her guidance counselor as often as her regular teachers, she will probably have important contact with her counselor, and that means her counselor will probably have a different perspective on your teen's social and academic development. It's important, therefore, to establish a relationship with your child's guidance counselor early in the school year. Make it a point to visit the guidance counselor's office at least a few times if things are going well and more often if your teen is having particular difficulties with school or is struggling with a difficult situation at home, such as a new step-parent. While you're there, browse through the parenting books and career guides available in the parent resource center.

BE OPEN AND SUPPORTIVE AS YOUR TEEN EXPLORES CAREER INTERESTS

IF you think back to your adolescence, you may remember how many different career goals you entertained over the years, and how, now that you're older, you can understand why your parents may have cringed when you told them some of your aspirations—or why you never bothered to tell them in the first place. It's important that your teen be willing to talk to you about *any* potential career goal, and the way to be sure your teen will share his aspirations is to be open and supportive of your teen's career interests. Here's how:

Let your teen's interests lead the way. Remember that you're discussing your teen's career, not your own. You may envision a particular future for your child, but you have to let *him* decide what he'll do once he graduates. Pushing too hard in one direction will often backfire, for your teen will resent your attempt to control his future. Remember that he's a developing individual with his own unique interests, talents, and aptitudes, and keep in mind that his career interests are likely to change several times before graduation. Remember, too, that it's important for your teen to discover on his own reasons why a particular career may not be so good for him, after all.

Talk with your teen about your job to help him begin to understand the connections between home and work and to consider the impact that work will have on all areas of his life. Describe what you do and why you do it. What's your day like? What kinds of decisions do you have to make? What impact do you have in your workplace and in society? How does your work affect your life at home? What are the benefits and drawbacks of your position? Why did you choose it? What would your ideal job be like, and why? Talking with your teen in this manner will also help your teen develop a sense of what kind of work would give him the greatest overall satisfaction.

Help your teen make choices that will get her closer to her career goals. If she plans to go to college, make sure she keeps her grades up and takes college preparatory classes. Promote good study habits and encourage your teen to get involved in extracurricular activities related to her interests.

But Dad, I Don't *Want* to Go to College . . .

What if you really want your teen to go to college, but your teen is set on being a baseball star? Remind your teen that the two are not mutually exclusive. It can't hurt your teen to have a degree—but it can hurt him if he doesn't. He can play baseball in college and maybe end up in the big leagues, but if he doesn't make it, or if he suffers a career-ending injury, he'll have another career to fall back on because of his education. In other words, he doesn't have to choose; he can do both.

PLANNING FOR COLLEGE

IF your teen plans to go to college, the time to take action is *now*. Here are some specific steps to take for the college bound:

➤ **Start saving now**, even if you think you don't have enough money to save. A little bit of money saved each month over several years can make a big dent in college costs, so examine your spending and expenses carefully. Do you spend an extra $2 a day on coffee? Could you carpool to save money on gas and maintenance? Could you shop more wisely by using coupons or watching for sales?

➤ Make sure your teen is taking **college preparatory classes** and continues to do so throughout high school.

➤ Encourage your teen to **participate in extracurricular activities**. This will help her explore and expand her interests and help her become a more well-rounded individual. It will also make her a more attractive candidate to college admissions officers.

➤ Emphasize the **importance of earning good grades**. A high grade point average will give your teen more options when it comes time to choose a college, and it will significantly improve your child's chances of earning a scholarship.

➤ **Don't let financial worries stop you** from considering college for your teen. There are billions of dollars available in scholarships and financial aid. Pay particular attention to scholarships and tuition discounts offered by local state and community colleges.

Many students and parents think that grades and SAT scores are the biggest factors for admission to college. In fact, these things are just one part of what we look at. While academics is a central element of college, it is not the only element. A college looks for students who will contribute socially, athletically, artistically, *and* academically to a school.

—JANE BRADFORD, ADMISSIONS OFFICER, SAN JOSE, CALIFORNIA

SUMMARY

THOUGH graduation is still four years off, it's not too early for eighth graders to begin thinking seriously about careers—in fact, career education in middle school can make a big difference to a teen who sees career options as limited by gender, socioeconomic status, or stereotypes. Today's middle school career education focuses on helping teens identify their interests, skills, and aptitudes; discover a wide range of career options; develop tentative career goals; and understand the social value of life work.

To enhance your teen's career education, discuss various career and college options with your teen, including two- and four-year colleges and specialized schools; help your teen identify his interests, strengths, and aptitudes; expose your teen to the incredible variety of possible occupations she can choose from; consult with your teen's guidance counselor; and encourage your teen to explore his career interests, even if those interests are not in line with your expectations.

After all, there are few choices in life more significant than choosing your life's work. Your support will help your teen make a career choice that will bring her life-long satisfaction.

General Career Categories with Sample Job Titles:

- ➤ administrative/support: secretary, administrative assistant, stenographer, transcriptionist
- ➤ arts/design: filmmaker, architect, painter, playwright, novelist, graphic designer
- ➤ business/finance: accountant, stock broker
- ➤ communications: writer/reporter, newscaster, speech writer, editor
- ➤ computers/technology: computer programmer, system analyst, information systems manager, Web page developer
- ➤ education: teacher, principal, guidance counselor, teaching assistant, test developer
- ➤ environmental: national park guide, conservationist
- ➤ health care/medical: doctor, dentist, physical therapist, radiologist, pharmacist, lab technician
- ➤ hospitality: hotel manager, chef, hair stylist, flight attendant, retail clerk
- ➤ legal: lawyer, judge, paralegal
- ➤ performance: singer, actor, song writer, dancer
- ➤ public service: politician
- ➤ retail: store manager, customer service representative, buyer, window dresser
- ➤ science/engineering: biologist, botanist, genetic engineer, civil engineer, meteorologist
- ➤ social services: social worker, career counselor, speech therapist
- ➤ trade/manufacturing: plumbing, construction, electronics, welder, machinist, truck driver, quality control inspector, foreman

The Best "Stuff" for 8th Graders and Their Parents

BY THE eighth grade, your teen will continue to develop his own tastes. He might have a favorite author, or genre, but as this book proves, a parent needs to encourage his interests and even introduce him to new ones. To make that task a little easier, we have compiled a list of the best books, magazines, CD-ROMs, and websites for your child. These are arranged by category. Remember, this is only a sample of many great resources available, and keep in mind your child's preferences.

BOOKS

THE following is a mixture of some old favorites and some new classics. They can all be found at your local library or at the neighborhood bookstore. The reading level of these books is fairly standard for eighth grade, although you may find that your teen is reading below or even above the level of these titles. Don't be concerned, as long as your teen is reading and learning, he's on the right track.

Autobiographies

All I Really Need to Know I Learned in Kindergarten, by Robert Fulghum (Ivy, 1993)

Anne Frank: The Diary of a Young Girl, by Anne Frank (Amercon, 1967)

Black Boy, by Richard Wright (Buccaneer, 1945)

I Know Why the Caged Bird Sings, by Maya Angelou (Bantam, 1983)

Fiction

After the Rain, by Norma Fox Mazer (Flare, 1997)

Bury Me Deep, by Christopher Pike (Archway, 1991)

Don't Look Behind You, by Lois Duncan (Laurel Leaf, 1990)

Ethan Frome, by Edith Wharton (Signet Classic, 1940)

Gentlehands, by M. E. Kerr (HarperTrophy, 1990)

Here's to You, Rachel Robinson, Judy Blume (Laurel Leaf, 1995)

Hoops, by Walter Dean Myers (Laurel Leaf, 1983)

Jacob Have I Loved, by Katherine Paterson (Ty Crowell, 1980)

Murder on the Orient Express, by Agatha Christie (Harper, 1934)

Nectar in a Sieve, by Kamala Markandaya (Penguin, 1954)

Runner, by Cynthia Voight (Fawcett, 1986)

The Call of the Wild, by Jack London (1903)

The Chocolate War, by Robert Cormier (Laurel Leaf, 1974)

The House on Mango Street, by Sandra Cisneros (Vintage, 1985)

The Human Comedy, by William Saroyan (Dell, 1944)

The Kidnapping of Christina Lattimore, by Joan Lowery Nixon (Laurel Leaf, 1992)

The Language of Goldfish, by Zibby Oneal (Puffin, 1990)

The Moves Make the Man, by Bruce Brooks (HarperTrophy, 1984)

The Outsiders, by S.E. Hinton (Puffin, 1967)

The Old Man and the Sea, by Ernest Hemingway (Scribner, 1953)

The Pigman, by Paul Zindel (Bantam Starfire, 1983)

The Red Badge of Courage, by Stephen Crane (1895)

Things Fall Apart, by Chinua Achebe (Anchor, 1994)
Tiger Eyes, by Judy Blume (Laurel Leaf, 1982)
To Kill a Mockingbird, by Harper Lee (Warner, 1960)
Violet and Claire, by Francesca Lia Block (HarperCollins, 1998)
We All Fall Down, by Robert Cormier (Laurel Leaf, 1993)
Where the Red Fern Grows, by Wilson Rawls (Bantam, 1961)

Plays

Romeo and Juliet, by William Shakespeare (any edition)
A Raisin in the Sun, by Lorraine Hansberry (Vintage, 1959)

Sci-Fi Fanatics

Wizards and warlords, robots and aliens—this is the stuff science fiction and fantasy are made of, and these two genres are likely to be especially appealing to your teen. And for good reason. Science fiction explores visions of the future—a future that is increasingly important and real to your teen. Fantasy literature often features coming of age stories in which the heroes and heroines must come to terms with themselves and find the special gift that will enable them to defeat the evil powers. In both science fiction and fantasy literature, the heroes are often "misfits" who gain inner strength and acceptance by their peers, and many stories help teens with their intellectual development by presenting interesting moral dilemmas. So if your teen is a *Star Trek* or *Star Wars* fanatic, if your teen consumes science fiction and fantasy stories like newspaper in a fire, relax. Your teen has found a healthy and stimulating hobby—one that he shares with millions of other adolescents.

Science Fiction/Fantasy

A Wizard Of Earthsea, by Ursula Le Guin (Bantam Spectra, 1984)
A Wrinkle in Time, by Madeleine L'Engle (Yearling, 1962)
Animal Farm, by George Orwell (Signet, 1946)
Child of the Owl, by Lawrence Yep (HarperTrophy, 1990)

Dragonsong, by Anne McCaffrey (Bantam Spectra, 1977)

Fahrenheit 451, by Ray Bradbury (Ballantine, 1953)

Flowers for Algernon, by Daniel Keyes (Skylark, 1966)

Hanging Out with Cici, by Francine Pascal (Pocket, 1978)

Harry Potter books, by J. K. Rowling (Scholastic, 1998–2001)

Life, the Universe and Everything, by Douglas Adams (Ballantine, 1995)

Lord of the Rings, by J.R.R. Tolkien (Houghton Mifflin, 1937)

Remembering the Good Times, by Richard Peck (Laurel Leaf, 1986)

Robot Dreams, by Isaac Asimov (Ace, 1994)

The Blue Sword, by Robin McKinley (Ace, 1991)

The Hobbit, by J.R.R. Tolkien (1937)

The Lion, the Witch and the Wardrobe, by C.S. Lewis (HarperCollins, 1950)

Watership Down, by Richard Adams (Avon, 1978)

MAGAZINES

Reading is a skill your teen will need for the rest of her life, and the best way to becoming a better reader is simply to read, everyday. If you find your teen isn't one for long novels, encourage her to read a magazine. There are plenty out there, and they will not only hold her attention, but also allow her to explore new subjects.

Boys' Life
This is a great general interest magazine for boys. Read about a wide variety of topics.

Creative Kids
Appropriately named, this magazine is meant to encourage your teen's creativity.

Cricket
This is a general interest magazine with stories, recipes, science articles, and games.

Dig
Does your teen want to be an archaeologist? *Dig* is a perfect magazine for her. Mummies, dinosaurs, and ancient civilizations fill its pages.

Explore!

This magazine sets out to answer the question "How does the world work?" There are plenty of adventure, science, and technology stories from all over the world.

Girls' Life

This magazine has plenty of advice, stories, celebrity interviews, and other topics of interest for girls.

Kid's Wall Street News

Show me the money! This magazine is a great introduction to saving, investing, and learning about the economy.

National Geographic World

With great articles about wildlife and world cultures, this award-winning magazine is perfect for pleasure reading.

Sports Illustrated for Kids

Have your teen sports fanatic check out *Sports Illustrated for Kids* and read all about his favorite teams, players, and sports events!

Teen Voices

A great magazine written by and for teen girls that focuses on real-life topics.

Time for Kids

From the editors of *Time* comes this current events magazine filled with great articles, photos, and maps.

WEBSITES

At the time of publication, the websites listed here were current. Due to the ever-changing nature of the Web, we cannot guarantee their continued existence or content. Parents should always supervise their children while they are on the Internet.

Much Ado About Chatting

You may have noticed that your teen loves to spend hours logged on the computer "chatting" with her friends. Chatting is when two or more people can send messages instantly through the Internet. Some chat rooms are set up to discuss a certain topic, for example, the Backstreet Boys, and some chat rooms are set up for people with a common background, for example a chat room for teens. While this sounds like a great way for your child to communicate with people all over the country and the world, there is a danger factor. Without face-to-face contact, people in the chat rooms can pretend to be anyone. For example, while it may seem harmless that your daughter is chatting with a teenage boy, it may be that the "teen" boy is actually a grown man using the Internet to hide his real intentions. Unfortunately, this is a growing problem. Make sure that you know what your teen is chatting about, and with whom. Teach your teen NEVER to give out personal information in chat rooms (name, age, address, phone number) and NEVER to arrange an in-person meeting with anyone that they "met" on the Internet. Don't hesitate to regulate your teen's time on the computer, and don't be afraid to ask who, what, where, when, and why? to your teen.

If you want more information to teach your child how to be safe, check out www.chatdanger.com or www.getnetwise.com, both are online sources for information about safety on the Internet.

Homework Help

Are you looking for a way to make homework more interesting for your teen? Visit these great sites with your teen to find materials to help him with his work.

www.bjpinchbeck.com
   This site, now hosted on Discovery.com, was created by B.J. and his father. This is a great portal to hundreds of sites dedicated to helping students complete their homework, and to learn something new.
www.bigchalk.com
   Formerly HomeworkCentral.com, BigChalk now encompasses resources for students, parents, and teachers. If your child needs

help with homework, he can find help that is both grade and subject specific.

Reference Guides

In eighth grade your child will be asked to complete assignments that require research. The Internet is a great place to gain access to excellent reference sites, such as the ones listed below.

www.brittanica.com
> This site offers free access to Britannica Encyclopaedias as well as a wealth of other reference sites.

http://kids.infoplease.com
> At Infoplease, students not only have access to a homework center, but there is a variety of almanacs, dictionaries, and encyclopedias.

Teen Interest

www.hotpopcorn.com
> If your teen loves movies, music, and television this is a great site for him to sound-off. Teens can write their own reviews of movies, as well as get all the latest entertainment news.

www.exploratorium.edu
> The famous San Francisco museum by the same name hosts this site. The museum is dedicated to science, art, and human perception. Here you will find exhibitions from the museum, activities, and resources for projects.

http://kids.msfc.nasa.gov
> NASA is sure to find some new recruits for the space program from this site! Complete with space art, space stories, and games, this site will keep children captivated for hours.

www.lacma.org
> The Los Angeles County Museum of Art features works of art online. There is also a feature that allows your teen to offer his opinion about a work of art.

www.metmuseum.org

New York's Metropolitan Museum of Art features 5,000 years of artwork. This is an amazing site that will allow your child to learn about art and artists throughout history.

www.surfmonkey.com

The content on this site is sure to please your eighth grader. Their wonderful links are organized by categories such as playful, artsy, brainy, spacey, newsworthy, techie, worldly, and starstruck.

http://teens-online.studentcenter.org/

This site has plenty of teen friendly content, including chat rooms, advice, and entertainment news.

www.worldbook.com

Head straight for World Book's Fun and Learning page. There you will find games, news, and even a Cyber Camp complete with a summer's worth of activities.

www.yahooligans.com

From the creators of Yahoo, comes Yahooligans, a web guide designed for kids and teens. Topics included are sports, around the world, and arts and entertainment.

Teen Issues

www.awarefoundation.org

The Adolescent Wellness and Reproductive Education (AWARE) Foundation's mission is educating and empowering adolescents to make responsible decisions regarding their wellness, sexuality, and reproductive health.

www.thefoundry.org/~girlnet/

One of the missions of this site is to inspire confidence and leadership in young women in relation to technology.

Television Programming

If you are like most households in the United States, you are watching dozens of hours of television every week. Here are some helpful hints:

1. Avoid programs that are geared exclusively toward selling a product.
2. Find programs that have a message, either moral or educational.
3. Talk with your teen after watching a program. Discuss the events of the story, how the characters behaved, you can even talk about the commercials they showed.
4. Steer your teen to programming that challenges him to think, feel, or communicate. Television should not be time to vegetate.
5. Seek programming that is both educational and entertaining. Believe it or not, there are quality programs out there.

Some stations that have plenty of educational programming are Animal Planet, The Discovery Channel, The History Channel, The Learning Channel, PBS, and The Travel Channel.

CD-ROMs

Not all parents are familiar with computers or how much technology improves daily. Thankfully, you and your child can benefit from these advances. CD-ROMs are a great alternative to video games, the Internet, and television. The materials found on CD-ROM are multimedia, your child will be able to see pictures, watch videos, and listen to recordings. Below are some of the best CD-ROMs we have found. They are arranged by subject.

Science

The New Way Things Work
     This CD-ROM is a great way to learn about machines and inventions that changed the world. Cost: $24.99
Night Sky Interactive
     Learn all about planets, stars, and comets with this interactive software. There is animation and narration. Cost: $19.99

Language

Rosetta Stone Spanish Explorer
Help your teen learn or improve his Spanish with this quality program complete with native speakers as teachers. Cost: $19.99
Rosetta Stone French Explorer
Parlez vous francais? Your teen may be studying French this year, so give him the help he needs with this fun interactive program. Cost: $19.99

Social Studies

Masks: Faces of the Pacific
This CD-ROM is a unique alternative to most programs. Learn about the history and culture surrounding the masks from the Pacific Rim. Cost: $19.99
History of the World 2.0
Complete with biographies, histories, and articles this program is a must for history buffs. Cost: $29.99

Music

Magix Music Maker 2000
If your teen is always composing music, give him the tools to do it right on the computer. This program is perfect for a budding composer. Cost: $26.99

PARENTS

Websites

There is a lot to know about your teen and his education. For this reason, we are offering websites with content that is both informative and interactive. Not only can you read articles about topics of interest, but also you can post your own ideas, and ask questions from the experts.

www.bigchalk.com

This site is a great resource not only for parents and children, but also for teachers and educators. You can search by subject, grade level, as well as by topic.

www.ed.gov

The U.S. Department of Education hosts this site to present accurate and complete information to parents regarding education in the United States.

www.familyeducation.com

This site offers information on your teen's development through the years, family activities, family news and topics, tips and resources, software downloads, message boards, ideas from parents, and advice from familyeducation.com experts.

www.helpforfamilies.com

This wonderful and helpful site was developed by a psychologist to help parents handle problems and address issues that children encounter in school.

www.lightspan.com

Lightspan offers plenty of information on education and parenting issues. The site is divided by grade level so you can track your teen's progress through the years.

www.megaskills.org

Megaskills are the behaviors students need to succeed in school and beyond. Parents and students can learn about teaching confidence, teamwork, problem solving, and motivation.

www.parentsoup.com

Parentsoup is not only parent-friendly, but also extremely informative. You can search topics arranged by age group, and write to experts on a variety of topics.

www.parentteen.com

This is a great site that covers everything you need to know about living with and raising a teenager.